IT'S F...
BUT NOT AS WE...

Eddie Russell FMI

Flame Ministries International
-Feeding the Poor in Spirit-

Head Office: Suite 6, 186 Hay Street, Subiaco,
Western Australia 6008
Postal Address: PO BOX 8133, Subiaco East, Western Australia 6008
Phone: +61 8 9382 3668
Email: faithjim@flameministries.org
Web: www.flameministries.org

1

IT'S FAITH JIM - BUT NOT AS WE KNOW IT

Imprimatur: ● Archbishop Barry J Hickey DD, OAM
Catholic Archdiocese of Perth,
Western Australia

Nihil obstat: Rev Fr Brian G O'Loughlin JCD, PhD,
Vicar General, Catholic Archdiocese of
Perth, Western Australia

Published by: *Flame Ministries International*
Printed in Perth, Western Australia by Scott Print

ISBN 0-646-44975-3

Dedications

- Our Lady of Guadalupe -
Mesoamerica, the New World, 1521.
The capital city of the Aztec empire falls under the Spanish forces.
Less than 20 years later, 9 million of the inhabitants of the land
who professed for centuries a polytheistic and human
sacrificing religion convert to Christ due to
Mary appearing to *(now Saint)* Juan Diego.
In the image on his tilma, Mary is standing on the moon
and in front of the sun wearing a black bow around her waist.
To the Aztec Indians, the black bow signifies that a
woman is pregnant - Mary was pregnant with Jesus.

Violet D'Cruz and daughters April and June Min Din

My late mother and father
- Sarah Anne & Fredrick Henry Alvin -

Thank you.

Special Thanks

– Kay Ford FMI –

Perth, Western Australia.
For being there for me as a special friend
when I needed to clarify my thoughts
whilst writing this book.
Your proofreading has been invaluable.

IT'S FAITH JIM - BUT NOT AS WE KNOW IT

- Table of Contents -

"The task of faith is to find the will of God, and then bring that will to fruition. If this requires an act that does violence to all natural law, or ordinary physical limitations, then faith is ready for the challenge."
-Ken Chant. Vision College Ltd.-

ABOUT THE AUTHOR

 EDDIE RUSSELL founded Flame Ministries International, a Canonical Evangelistic Organisation in the Archdiocese of Perth, Western Australia in 1990 and serves as a Senior Director.

He is an officially commissioned lay Catholic evangelist conferred by the Most Rev Barry James Hickey, Archbishop of the Catholic Archdiocese of Perth, Western Australia who also accepted Eddie's vows of obedience.

Before the formation of Flame Ministries International, he co-authored a 15-week Bible Seminar called Set My People on Fire that was to form the basis of Flame Ministries International's biblical ethic upon its formation. Later that year, the Holy Spirit inspired Eddie with the vision for Flame Ministries itself.

The vision accepted by the authors of Set My People on Fire established the ministry, and since that time, the seminar has functioned in Perth and England with segments in other states of Australia, Malaysia and Singapore and has had delegates participating using DVD, CD or audio tape by correspondence in Australia, England, New Zealand, Alaska and the U.S.A.

With the approval and acceptance of local Ordinaries, Eddie has been the keynote speaker for major national conferences, evangelisation outreaches, retreats, parish and revival missions in Australia, Malaysia,

Singapore, Indonesia, England, Portugal, Africa, Mexico and the USA in both Catholic and non-Catholic Churches where his ministry has drawn people in the thousands.

Invited to Mexico in 2002 by the Director for the Commission of the Doctrine of Faith to preach on the Baptism of Fire around the country of Mexico, Norberto Cardinal Rivera Carrera, Archbishop Primado de Mexico, officially welcomed him and the Archbishop's letter of welcome read out by the presenter on national television.

During that mission, Eddie was invited by Claravision Catholic Television in Mexico City to preach a live two-hour broadcast on The Baptism of Fire, which has now spread in many countries around the world and the prophecy that began it at his Praise Meeting in Perth on May 13th 1993.

The show was so popular an invitation came to do a second live broadcast a week later. Both shows broadcast to an audience of 25 million people throughout Latin South America, Mexico, USA, Canada and Alaska and were very successful. During the broadcasts, many people and priests rang the stations asking how they too could receive the Baptism of Fire.

Involved with the Catholic Charismatic Renewal in Perth for over twenty-five years, most of which has been in leadership, Eddie also founded the St. Mary's Cathedral Praise Meeting in the City of Perth during 1990 where he still serves as the leader today - the meeting functions as an outreach of Flame Ministries International.

Eddie represents the Praise Meeting on the Archdiocesan Catholic Charismatic Renewal Leaders body and represents Flame Ministries International as a member of the State Service Committee of the Catholic Charismatic Renewal of Western Australia.

In addition, Eddie has also written several Bible seminars and challenging articles published to over fourteen countries with some translated into several languages.

The internationally popular English edition of his book, 12 Steps to Divine Healing, has sold in many countries around the world. Testimonials regarding healing, and blessings received by those that have read it continue to be reported.

The German publication is available in Christian bookstores in all German-speaking countries. Other translations are in Slovenian, Croatian, Portuguese and Spanish.

Committed to the Great Commission, Eddie devotes his life to the proclamation of the Gospel in the spirit of Ad Gentes.

I have written this book in response to many requests from people who have read my book 12 Steps to Divine Healing; it covers faith as a charism, a law, a gift, a grace, a natural endowment, and even, a science.

The title of this book is a parody on the original Star-Trek famous line, "It's life Jim - But not as we know it" and approaches the cosmogony of faith in Hebrews 11:1-3. Consequently it attempts to go boldly where no man has gone before, and hence the title, "It's Faith Jim - But not as we know it."

In the first three verses of Hebrews 11 is the whole mystery of faith regarding exactly what it is and how *we understand and know by faith* that the Word of God creates the universe.

The author of Hebrews does not elaborate on this cosmic event and promptly gives examples from history. We can assume that because there are no elaborations the Christians of the day knew exactly what he meant. The question the book approaches is, do we?

From this standpoint, I have presented how the Mazzaroth reveals God's salvation plan written in the constellations and how the corruption at Babel gave birth to the modern day occult zodiac with Biblical references and astronomical calculations to show what people saw in the heavens at that time.

It also explains the relationship between the Logos and the Rhema in the work of creation, salvation, and the miraculous events revealed in the lives of Adam through to Jesus and, for us today.

Investigating the dust from which God formed Adam, it approaches the creation of the universe and humanity from a sub-atomic level and asks, "Was Adam sub-atomic dust that speaks?"

This book is not a complete exegesis on faith, or indeed a complete cosmogony or cosmology even if it does have an Aristotelian metaphysical nature, but rather its purpose is to approach the nature of faith itself in a practical way that we can apply in daily life

Since this book is not only concerned with the beginning, but also with the end of creation, its foundation is on the premise that God, although fully involved in it, is separate from it. In these regards, its cosmogony could be in the area of the Scholastics Hylomorphism; however, I only discovered these probabilities after setting out my thoughts.

Its cosmology and cosmogony if anything, are relating to the comments in the Letter to the Hebrews regarding understanding the origin of the universe by the Word of God.

Because this is so powerfully connected in Hebrews chapter eleven verse three, we cannot approach the subject of faith without approaching the universe itself.

Faith is a gift supernaturally infused by God but it is also a law that needs application in order to have its

11

effect. The book attempts to explain that law in a simple to understand way, giving numerous practical examples as well as inspiring personal testimonies, and explains how a Rhema word spoken in faith can activate a dead body.

It also explains how this can consecrate bread and wine and how it affects the Incarnation, the New Adam and the New Eve opening up the revelation of Christ at Cana as well as bringing a physical body into a purely spiritual realm without breaking spiritual or natural laws. It also explains how faith comes, grows, and achieves results and explains how we can apply it in our daily life.

Written from the heart of the Evangelist whose primary motivation is to bring encounter with Jesus and conviction of his truth rather than education alone, this book seeks to make Jesus known to the glory of God and to inspire faith in him that shared with others it will bring them salvation.

It is therefore a book for the everyday person to apply effectively in daily life. However, to find out more and gain a complete knowledge about faith, read the best book ever written on the subject, the Bible.

I pray this book will bless my readers with an increase of faith in Jesus Christ and an absolute trust in the efficacy of the Word of God.

Eddie Russell FMI

Chapter 1

Lord, increase our faith

"Faith is the realisation of what is hoped for and evidence of things not seen. Because of it, the ancients were well attested. By faith we understand that the universe was ordered by the word of God so that what is visible came to be through the invisible."
Hebrews 11:1-3.

One day, Jesus' disciples asked him to increase their faith. Jesus told them that if their faith was only the size of a mustard seed, they could speak to a mulberry tree that would obey them and be uprooted and planted into the sea. *(Luke 17:5-10)*

Again, when his disciples could not cast out a demon *(Matthew 17:14-21)* Jesus only told them that if they had faith the size of a mustard seed, they could speak to a mountain telling it to move from here to there and it will move, and nothing would be impossible for them; he offers no more explanations.

Throughout his ministry, we see Jesus responding positively to faith and making specific mention when he grants the answer to people's requests or actions. To his disciples however, he does not say to them, as he would to others, "Be it done according as your faith" or, "your faith has saved you." Could it be because, unlike the Roman Centurion or the Canaanite woman, who had no covenant rights and were enemies of the Jews, received what they asked by faith, that Jesus did not see faith in the disciples?

On the other hand, was there another reason for this strange response that renders us, his modern day disciples, somewhat perplexed at such a short answer wondering where it leaves us?

To make matters worse for those of us who do not understand, the Letter to the Hebrews adds to our bewilderment in chapter 11:1, by saying that, *"Faith is the realisation of what is hoped for and evidence of things not seen."* Well, at least we now know what it is; it is obviously the realisation of hope and the evidence of things not seen!

However, understanding this seemingly enigmatic contradiction is another problem altogether for many of us. Rather than give us a more in-depth explanation of this statement, the Letter immediately mentions the cosmic dimensions of faith and lists off all the great men and women in the Old Testament who had accomplished amazing things by and through this mystery called faith as a foregone conclusion. Presumably, the Hebrews knew exactly what the Epistle meant by faith as described and therefore the author had no need to elaborate other than to give some practical examples.

In Hebrews, the first practical example is that faith and the Word of God reveals the origin of the universe; *"We know by faith that the universe was ordered by the word of God so that what is visible came to be through the invisible."* And it continues to say that their ancestors were well attested because of their faith and *we* understand *by faith* that the universe was ordered by the Word of God and therefore, what was visible came into being through the invisible.

It seems reasonable to acknowledge this comment as one not entirely ignorant of some understanding of the zodiac or astronomy since the origin of the universe gains such an important mention. Nor was it merely knowledge based on a religious concept; the Cabalistic Magi had been around for a long time and the study and knowledge of the zodiac was well established; all the pagan nations around them either lived by or studied the constellations.

Now hidden by occult corruption, God's redemptive plan in the heavens is never the less clear for all to see "The heavens declare the Glory of God and firmament proclaims the builders craft." *(Psalm 19:1-2)* God even taunts Job about this when he said to him, "Have you fitted a curb to the Pleiades, or loosened the bonds of Orion? Can you bring forth the Mazzaroth in their season, or guide the Bear with its train? Do you know the ordinances of the heavens; can you put into effect their plan on the earth?" *(Job 38:31-33)* Obviously, God did, and calls them by name.

The question for us is do *we* really understand this. Because if we do, then there's no need for me to write this book and no need for you to be reading it right now to find out. In which case there is also no need to explain the origin of the universe and how it began because we all know by faith exactly how that happened. Unless of course, you have put your faith in a Big Bang Theory the same way that Darwin put his faith in his own supposition that we humans originated on the planet of the apes, which the earth would have been if in fact we had come from apes in the first place.

Amazingly, so many people have put their faith in Darwin's personal supposition to such a degree that they have evolved a mere theory into scientific fact and miraculously did it without any tangible proof or evidence. In fact, you have to have real faith to do that and believe it because you simply cannot see how they did it!

Which then is easier to understand, science or faith? Maybe we could suggest that science is easier for those who do not understand faith and look to science for the answers to the mystery of life. That seems more reasonable to them and therefore easier to believe. It is certain however that

15

they and science itself will inevitably come to the same conclusion as Albert Einstein when he said, "God is subtle."

As far as the creation of the universe is concerned, it makes more sense to accept by faith that the Word of God creates it; God's Word was there in the beginning with God and all things came to be through him including life according to John 1:1-3. Why is this so? It is so because to have a Big Bang *Theory*, you need something to bang it! The law of physics determines that there had to be *matter* in the first place. This in turn means that *something* existed enabling *something* else to bang into it. So now, we have to ask ourselves where, could that have come from.

The solution proposed by some in the scientific community is that before the Big Bang there was nothing and that is where time began. This is a strange notion since the Bang itself being matter needed an origin in order for it to bang. Therefore, it seems logical to accept God as the origin of the Bang even if the Bang is in fact what happens as theorised. It seems certain that science will eventually agree with faith that God is the originator of life and the Creator of the universe and in spite of itself, science will become the evidence of what faith accepts without it.

The Letter to the Hebrews is a huge subject regarding how the Word of God formed the constellations and it would take another book to do it justice. However, it seems expedient to include at least an overview to grasp a little better the possible reasons why the letter does not elaborate on the statement, *"By faith we understand that the universe was ordered by the Word of God, so that what is visible came into being through the invisible."*

Understanding a little about the Mazzaroth, a Hebrew word meaning, *the crowns*, or *the constellations*, as well as how the Word of God operated and ordered the universe will help us to grasp why the Hebrews needed no instruction on what the author meant by that statement when he taught on faith as both seem intricately and essentially connected.

The reason there is no explanation was likely because they were familiar with the constellations and the letter was to give them courage in the midst of their persecution after the frightening death of James; they understood why those great men and women of God *(the ancients)* could accomplish what they did.

They understood that it was not a *blind* faith that achieved such miraculous results, but a faith based on the Word of God and his revelation of the Mazzaroth from the scriptural viewpoint rather than the Cabbalistic Magi, Greek, Roman, Arabian and Egyptian cosmologies as well as others with which they were familiar. This was either because they were converts from those backgrounds or because they knew Jewish history in this regard as well as the teachings of the Talmud.

To grasp the importance of Hebrews 11:3, the first thing we need to establish is the meaning of the word, *Word* upon which both faith and the creation of the universe exists and operates. We also need understanding of our own human nature in relation to faith and the Word made flesh before we approach the origin and the meaning of universe itself, and so we will approach that in the next chapter.

Chapter 2

The Word: The Logos and Rhema are one

The English language has only one word for word and that is, *word*. In Greek *(the original language of the Epistles)*, there are two words for word, which are, *Logos* and *Rhema* and so it is important when reading the Bible to know which Greek word is used in the English translation to understand the meaning of the text as the writer intended. Logos means, to counsel, reason, or to assess truth and it specifically refers to Jesus in John's Gospel. Rhema means, a word spoken.

Revealing a cosmogony relating to the Word of God, Saint John begins his Gospel saying, "In the beginning was the Word, and the Word was with God, and the Word was God. He was in the beginning with God. All things came to be through him, and without him, nothing came to be. What came to be through him was life and this life was the light of the human race; the light shines in the darkness and the darkness has not overcome it." John continues, "He was in the world, *and the world came to be through him…* and the Word became flesh."

The word Genesis means Beginning or Personified Pre-existence. In the beginning, there is only God and nothing existed in the created order. Therefore, God is *uncreated*, meaning that no one created God; He is, or as he would say of himself, "I Am." We accept from the Bible and doctrine that God is *Love,* and so it would be equally true to say that, God as he is in himself as God, is *Uncreated Love.* When God speaks, he brings forth from his uncreated self something that now exists in the created order.

The Word that speaks forth from God's uncreated self is his *creative love* that brings creation into existence: *Begotten of God.* It is also God's Creative Word and the Personified Pre-existence sent to accomplish exactly what God has said. *(John 3:16)* The action of the Word coming from God brings into existence exactly what the Word expresses, nothing more and nothing less; God is the Logos, and when the Logos speaks, it becomes Rhema. The Creative Word is the Rhema of God; the Personified Pre-Existence who is Christ, and it is in him that we live, move, and have our being and by which the whole universe is created.

In John's Gospel chapter one, verse one he says, "…and the Word was God," It would be easy to read this, as meaning that the word is, *God,* in other words, the word G-O-D. In fact, it really means that the *Word* is God, and they are one and exactly the same expression revealed as Logos and Rhema. Jesus is the Logos in human form sent by the Father that becomes Rhema through his speech and actions in his physical humanity. *(John 14:9-12; John 17:11)* Jesus tells us that the words he speaks come from the Father and to see him is to see the Father. He reflects perfectly the invisible God. *(John 5:24; John 5:30; John 6:45; John 6:63; John 8:31-32; John 8: 47)*

When St. John tells us, he was in the world and the world came to be through him, he is saying that Jesus is the Personified Pre-existing Rhema of God that brought everything into being when God spoke it in Genesis. When John says that he came to his own, but his people did not accept him, he is referring to the human genealogy of Jesus and the revelation in scripture that speaks exclusively of Jesus throughout biblical history.

His own are the twelve tribes of Israel; the Jews to whom the revelation of the Messiah had been told and who should have been the first to recognise him from the teachings of the Patriarchs and Prophets, but they did not. We can accept this as separate from creation since creation recognised him as we see when Jesus calmed the storm on the lake, walked on the sea and when he cured Peter's mother-in-law by addressing the fever, as just three examples.

Throughout the Creation Story in chapter one of the book of Genesis, we see the Word; the Logos translated from the Hebrew; *dabar* meaning creative word of God - YHWH forming the universe and all that it contains. God speaks nine times in the order of creation. (1) He *speaks* matter into existence. (2) He *speaks* light into existence. (3) He *speaks* the atmosphere into existence. (4) He *speaks* the lands into existence. (5) He *speaks* vegetation into existence (6) He *speaks* the heavenly bodies into existence (7) He *speaks* the birds and the fish into existence (8) He *speaks* all the land animals into existence and finally, (9) He *speaks* man *(Adam)* into existence and establishes him above all that he has created. These works of the Logos and Rhema, called the Hexaemeron signify a term of six days or, the history of the six days. On the seventh day, God rests and gives his divine approval.

At each order of creation we read, "Then God *said*." In other words, although not a language in the human sense, but rather an *act* of the Logos, God *spoke* creation into existence and *declared* it good. In this context, Logos is in respect to the mind alone - "A Greek philosopher named Heraclitus first used the term Logos around 600 B.C. to designate the divine reason or plan which coordinates a changing universe. This word was well suited to John's purpose in John 1.

St. Augustine studied more closely the analogy between the divine Word and human speech and drew from it teachings long accepted in Catholic theology. He compares the Word of God, not to the word spoken by the lips, but to the interior speech of the soul, whereby we may in some measure grasp the Divine mystery; engendered by the mind it remains therein, is equal thereto, and is the source of its operations." *(New Advent Catholic Encyclopaedia)* Later developed and enriched by St. Thomas Aquinas this doctrine appeared in his Summa Theologica.

Whatever God *said* came to be exactly as he *spoke* it; light was light and not just a simile of light for example. It is only when God creates man that his vocabulary changes, "Then God *said*, 'Let *us* make man in *our* image, after *our* likeness." Only in this particular order of his creation does God use the plural *us* and *our* as referring to himself when creating man. *(Genesis 1:26-27; Genesis 2:7)*

The Trinity is not specifically mentioned here but it is clear to see in both chapter one and chapter two of Genesis that God who is Spirit, refers to himself in the plural, speaks the Word and breaths a life-giving spirit into the man he has formed from the dust so that it becomes a living being. *(Genesis 2:7)* The Hebrew understanding of the title God *(Elohim)* means, a single God in whom there is a plurality of persons.

Although the Hebrews did not have the fullness of revelation as we do through Jesus Christ, it is implicit in their understanding of plurality; the word used for God in Genesis 1:1 is "Elohim," which is a form of the word "El." In the Hebrew language, the "im" ending imputes plurality. Therefore, "Elohim" is the plural form of the word "El." This plurality as we now understand through divine revelation is the Trinity: Father, Son and Holy Spirit. Therefore, the word

God reveals the Father *(Spirit)* the Son *(Word)* and the Holy Spirit *(Breath)*.

The Catechism of the Catholic Church explains that the Trinity is One. It teaches that we do not confess three Gods, but one God in three persons, the 'consubstantial Trinity.' The divine persons do not share the one divinity among themselves but each of them is God whole and entire: 'The Father is that which the Son is, the Son that which the Father is, the Father and the Son that which the Holy Spirit is, i.e. by nature one God...*253*

The divine persons are distinct from one another. God is one but not solitary. 'Father', 'Son', 'Holy Spirit' are not simply names designating modalities of the divine being, for they are distinct from one another. He is not the Father who is the Son, nor is the Son who is the Father, nor the Holy Spirit who is the Father and the Son. They are distinct from one another in their relations of origin. The Father who generates - the Son who is begotten and the Holy Spirit who proceeds. The divine Unity is Triune. *254*

The divine persons are relative to one another. Because it does not divide the divine unity, the real distinction of the persons from one another resides solely in the relationships, which relate them to one another. In the relational names of the persons, the Father is related to the Son, the Son to the Father, and the Holy Spirit to both.

While they are called three persons in view of their relations, we believe one nature or substance. Indeed, everything is one where there is no opposition of relationship. Because of that unity, the Father is wholly in the Son and wholly in the Holy Spirit; the Son is wholly in the Father and wholly in the Holy Spirit; the Holy Spirit is wholly in the Father and wholly in the Son. *256*

Saint Paul later teaches that we are tripartite beings made up of body, soul and spirit and this reflects the

Trinitarian divine image spoken of in Genesis 1:27. In other words, a human being is first a spirit being who has a soul and lives in a body and therefore, unlike the rest of his creation, God created man in his own image and likeness. *(1Thessolonians 5:23)* "And let them have dominion over" is God's word giving man total authority over all that God has made.

This authority is not only a statement of covenant exchange but also proper to man's integrity in the body for this is how he, as a spirit being, lives in the physical world of nature and as such, man is the sole agency of authority on earth. From this moment and until the end of the world God chose to work with and through man in the natural order; God brings creatures to Adam to see what he will name them. When the Logos in Adam *speaks* a *Rhema* name on earth, God the Logos *speaks* Rhema in heaven and it is so.

As we continue, we will see that our speech is integral to faith and the outcome of prayer, for in prayer we must give God permission to act. In brief, as we see throughout scripture, God seeks a human being that will cooperate with him in order for God to act on man's behalf in the earth. Moses is to set his people free from the slavery of Egypt as one example; God spoke to Moses and when he did, he created a new reality.

When Moses speaks as God instructed, God acts and the new reality comes into effect; Moses told Pharaoh there would be a plague and there was a plague sent by God and so on. This is the Logos operating as Rhema in Moses and we find this as a constant throughout the Bible. This culminates with God speaking as God in the man Jesus; The Word, the Logos, made flesh.

God and the Word are one and the power of our speech activates the faith that brings life, healing, liberty, salvation, prosperity and joy. It can also bring catastrophe for our lives if not understood. Speech is a constant principle of faith throughout the Bible. Speech is such a powerful force that it embodies faith for good or bad and we suffer the bad consequences or the blessings of our tongues when we use negative or positive speech even without knowledge of God.

Properly understood, prayer is perfect positive speech; true prayer expresses God's perfect and revealed will and agrees with his Word enshrined in the Bible; the Word of God. In this way, God's will is a reality on earth as it is in heaven.

Chapter 3

Adam – Was he Sub-Atomic dust that speaks?

It is interesting to note that God did not choose gold, diamonds, sapphires, or any other precious substance from which to create Adam *(Hebrew; Adam – the man)*. On the contrary, he chose the most seemingly unvalued and common substance, the dust of the earth *(Hebrew; adamah – the dust)*. If God had made Adam from gold or precious stones then that is what he would return to when he died.

Gold, as all the valuable jewels, are a product of what the earth has formed in its composition and mass over time. As scientific study advances, it seems that the dust could symbolise the base-origin of *matter* at a sub-atomic level including that of the precious metals and stones and indeed, that of the entire universe.

Although it is the commonly held belief that God took a handful of dirt and formed it into a man; an act of miraculous proportions made even more so by the fact that God took what seems to be of little value and trodden under foot and made it into his crowning glory; Adam. Never the less, it would seem that to create man from something other than the very substance of what forms all *matter* would make him far less than what he was destined to be in God's created order.

The basic element of our physical composition is carbon. It is the same with the physical creation; it turns to dust when carbon has been broken down either by fire or natural attrition. Carbon compressed at a very high degree becomes a diamond, but the diamond and the twig on a tree are exactly the same base element under different circumstances. We become dust when our body has decomposed and the 98% water has evaporated. However, the substance of what we call dust is still particles of *matter* that has a sub-atomic structure the same as all *matter*; the diamond and our flesh are the same effected by different circumstances. Hence, the notion proposed here is that the dust was not so much a handful of dirt but the very substance that forms the entire cosmos and created natural order.

From modern physics, we know that dust is not just dirt on the ground; once thought of as the smallest element, we now know that atoms have an even smaller sub-structure. According to Sub-Atomic Theory, the fundamental particles now consist of 6 lepton particles and 6 quark particles and a combination of quarks make up the other particles. An electron is still a fundamental particle, but protons and neutrons are combinations of quarks.

In August 2002, several newspapers reported that NASA'S Stardust spacecraft was collecting the first samples from a comet and had begun collecting cosmic dust and particles smaller than one-hundredth the width of a strand of human hair that are to be studied. The reports quoted Don Brownlee, professor of astronomy, who explained: "If you look at the Milky Way on a dark night, you may see a black band stretching along the centre. The band is interstellar dust blocking the light from distant stars. "These are the particles that Stardust will be collecting."

The professor, based at the University of Washington, Seattle, is the Stardust mission's principal investigator. He said the dust passes through the universe like wind and includes most elements in the periodic table.

In early 2004, the Stardust spacecraft collected particles up to 4.5 billion years old from the gas and dust that escaped from inside the comet Wild 2. Tom Duxbury, the project's manager at NASA's California-based Jet Propulsion Laboratory, said scientists would analyse those particles back on Earth. Stardust landed on January 15 2006. NASA says that the samples *(of cosmic dust)* "could yield important clues on the formation of the universe, as well as how life began on earth."

Saint Thomas Aquinas tells us that man's natural tendency is towards the good. This is the basic instinct of the divine image in man to seek his Creator in spite of that immediate knowledge removed by the sin of Adam. This urge remains as a powerful driving force that underpins man's natural ability to have faith and the capacity to seek truth through religion, philosophy, rational thought, or science.

The very fact that science seeks the truth of our existence by studying the smallest things imaginable is somewhat significant in that it reflects the innate compulsion in the heart of man to seek his origin even without faith in God. In the case of the NASA Stardust probe, it seeks cosmic dust in order to grapple with the mystery of how life began here on earth. This dust, once collected and analysed at a sub-atomic level will attempt to answer that eternal question.

When we consider that current sub-atomic theory has discovered elements smaller than the atom, one wonders how small it could get before it is understood that God is, as Albert Einstein once said, "subtle."

Perhaps this subtly can be more easily understood by faith; a faith of which Jesus said should be as that of a little child, than it can by science; the Letter to the Hebrews didn't need to elaborate on the origins of the universe to understand that it was the Word of God that had ordered it.

As science probes ever deeper into the mystery of the cosmos, it seems to confirm increasingly what we can understand by faith in God's Word. The wonderful thing is that science confirms faith by fact and becomes the *"evidence of what cannot be seen"*, and dare we say, "What we hope for."

Not spoken into existence as was the rest of creation makes the *dust* that formed Adam significant: the *dust* exists when God spoke it into existence with the rest of the cosmos, but it came into being in a particular way by God's own hand when he created Adam. In addition, this dust was the only life form created by God that received the breath of God as a life giving Spirit in order to animate it. This is the only act of God in his creation reflecting the *divine image*; an image endowed with the ability to know its Creator in a conscious and intelligent way.

Known and understood through the agency of the soul our conscious knowledge of God resides in the area of the intellect, emotions, and the will that animates us towards an intelligent love. This is not the same with other living creatures; unlike man, they cannot counsel, reason, or assess the truth in the same way in order to either seek or understand the source of their own existence or knowledge of God. Therefore, they cannot have faith because this is an attribute unique to us in order to know the mysteries of God even before we have the facts.

Adam's knowledge came from God directly from Spirit to spirit. He understood more directly in his soul than we do now due to original sin and therefore his actions in his physical body perfectly reflected the divine will. In other words, the *Logos* spoke the *Rhema* that created Adam. When the breath of God *(Spirit)* entered Adam, the divine image *(Logos)* in Adam also spoke *(Rhema)* naming all creatures. Because the Spirit and the Word agree, it was so according to God and that spoken on earth is so in heaven.

This was the case until the fall of Adam *(Genesis 3)* when that communication between man and God was broken through Adam's original sin; a sin reconciled and repaired by the Word *(Logos)* made flesh, Jesus Christ, the New Adam represented by the *leather* garment that God made with which to cloth them. *(Genesis 3:21)* Because God could not look upon the sin this was necessary so that God could continue to talk to Adam and Eve in preparation for the coming of the Lamb of God whose blood takes the sin away.

When faced with the death that original sin introduced, we cannot help but feel short-changed in some way, but even death is God's mercy. As an immortal soul created to live forever had death not come to Adam, he could have sinned continually and remained separated from God for eternity in a fallen physical nature and God's plan of redemption through the atoning death of Jesus Christ could not happen, whereas the sacrifice of Jesus on Calvary destroyed the final enemy that is death. Just as the cement at the edge of a pavement curbs the distinction from the road, so death is a curb that diminishes our life of sin - it says, thus far, and no more.

Even though we now understand far less than God intended due to Adam's sin, the instinct for everlasting life remains and thus our hunger for knowledge of the universe and indeed, life itself propels us forward either through faith or science, or both. However, God does not leave it there. He sends Jesus to speak the words of eternal life that whoever would believe in him would not perish. *(John 3:16)*

His words are spirit and truth; the spirit animates and the truth sets free.

Adam created from the literal dust of the earth or sub-atomic particles *(cosmic dust)* might seem debatable, and yet we know according the Bible that we are dust and to dust we shall return. At the first observation, this would be so because once the 98% of water in a body has evaporated it leaves the 2% dust or ash. However, the proposition here is that the substance of the 2% dust or ash has the same sub atomic structure as the rest of matter in the cosmos and so we return to our original state before the creation of Adam - the dust from which he came.

We, like Adam are sub atomic dust that speaks and in that speech are the only species that can contemplate God and speak to him and him to us, and because we are creatures of faith, we can not only know this but also understand it and give God the glory in what he has made.

Chapter 4

God's redemptive plan is clear in the stars for all to see

When God *said*, "Let there be" he spoke all creation into existence placing everything in its order and sequence. God is a God of order not confusion or random action, and so it is with everything that he does because he brought order out of chaos in the beginning.

Everything works in perfect harmony and balance, not one thing from the sub-atomic level to the entire universe rebels against its nature. The only exception is one thing and one thing only, our free will and it is in this area that we are supreme above all created things. The rebellious will of Adam caused sin and the subsequent corruption of the Mazzaroth so that we can now begin to understand it only by faith in the Word of God and even then only as through a dark glass.

God's Word in the Bible has revealed his plan of salvation written in the stars for all on earth to see. "Let there be lights in the dome of the sky, to separate day from night. Let them mark the fixed times, the days and the years." *(Genesis 1:14)* It is clear from this verse that it was God's plan to let the stars, constellations and planets fix the times, days and years of the earth so that we can follow his purposes in them.

Saint Paul refers to this passage as well as many others in the Psalms when he encourages the Roman Christians in his letter about the order of salvation and the wrath that awaits the disobedient when he says, "For what can be known about God is evident to them, because God has made it evident to them. Ever since the creation of the world, his invisible attributes of eternal power and divinity have been able to be understood and perceived in what he has made." *(Romans1:19-20)*

In other words, the invisible origin of the universe is evident through the visible universe that clearly reveals what is unseen by virtue of itself as the tangible evidence of its own origin and existence. Therefore, there is no excuse to say that God does not exist.

Psalm 19:1-6 further says that, "The heavens declare the glory of God; the sky proclaims the builders craft. One day to the next conveys that message; one night to the next imparts the knowledge. There is no sound; no voice heard; yet, their report goes forth, to the ends of the world. God pitched there a tent *(a tabernacle)* for the sun; it comes forth like a bridegroom from his chamber, and like an athlete joyfully runs its course."

The message the heavens declare is the one and only message that God has ever proclaimed and that is, the Gospel. There is no sound because the very existence of the universe is declaring God's glory for all to see.

The bridegroom is referring to Jesus for whom God has made a tabernacle in the heavens. Clearly understood from the Hebrew name, the term athlete is the strong man in this context and it refers to Jesus. In Malachi 3:20 we read, "But for you who fear my name, there will arise the sun of justice with its healing rays." This is referring to the coming Messiah: Jesus of Nazareth. Jesus is the Bridegroom in Matthew 25:6, Ephesians 5:21-32, and Revelations 21:2.

In Revelations 22:16-17 Jesus also refers to himself as, "The bright morning star." This is the sun revealed in the constellations and spoken of in Malachi 3:20. Psalm 33:6 says how this came to be, "By the Lord's word the heavens were made; by the breath of his mouth their entire host."

The host is referring to the constellations, the Hebrew word for which is, Mazzaroth. God speaks of the Mazzaroth when he challenges Job in chapter 38:31-33 saying, "Have you fitted a curb to the Pleiades, or loosened the bonds of Orion? Can you bring forth the Mazzaroth in their season, or guide the Bear with its train? Do you know the ordinances of the heavens; can you put into effect their plan on the earth?" From the very fact that God mentions it as a matter of course, we can assume that Job knows about the Mazzaroth. In addition, it is reasonable to assume that Job understood that the physical heavens show God's plans for the earth and that he should not by that virtue, doubt God's sovereign plan in his dealings with him.

The Hebrew word Mazzaroth means, *The Crowns*. The Mazzaroth is the Hebrew equivalent of the Greek and Latin word, *Zodiac*. The Mazzaroth is not astrology, but more accurately, astronomy. It is the occult corruption called the zodiac, which is astrology.

There are numerous references to the celestial bodies throughout the Bible and the author of Hebrews would have been familiar with them all. His readers, by virtue of being a Jew or converts from the Babylonian, Egyptian, Iranian or Greek backgrounds also knew the zodiac but now understood it from the point of view of the Mazzaroth. The Letter to the Hebrews addresses Gentile converts from pagan and other esoteric cabbalistic practices as well as Jewish converts that knew the history of the Mazzaroth. In the latter case, they would have understood that the word Mazzaroth came from the root word in

33

Hebrew, *Zodi*, which means, *The Way*. The early Christians gained the title, "Followers of the Way" because they were disciples of Jesus who is, "The Way." *(Acts9: 2, Acts 19:25-26, Acts 24:14 and 22)* As we begin to unfold the hidden message behind the zodiac, we will see how the Gospel fits into God's cosmological extravagance clearly showing that Jesus is *The Way*, The Truth, and The Life.

Acts 3:20-21 says, "And that the Lord may grant you times of refreshment and send you the Messiah already appointed for you, Jesus, whom heaven must receive until the times of universal restoration of which God spoke through the mouth of his prophets from ancient times."

This reflects the Canticle of Zechariah in Luke 1:69-70, "He has raised up a horn for our salvation within the house of David his servant, even as he promised through the mouth of his holy prophets from *ancient times*." Clearly revealed from the very beginning, ancient times, the horn refers to Jesus.

Again, it would have been no great mystery for these early Christians to understand Jesus as the sun mentioned in scripture as well as in the order of the constellations even though God's redemptive plan written in the stars was by now corrupted with the occult understanding of the zodiac established because of Nimrod at Babylon. Until then, the stars testified to their Creator and even inspired faith when understood to express God's design, but after Nimrod, the study of the stars in the form of the zodiac only inspired a fatalistic view of man's destiny.

Chapter 5

How God's redemption plan written in the stars was corrupted

atan has a counterfeit of everything that God has. The zodiac is his occult astrological corruption of the astronomy of the Mazzaroth intended to veil what God has made clear for all to see regarding his plan of salvation as we look into the sky on a clear night.

To grasp the point of the Letter to the Hebrews regarding the creation of the universe we need to trace Satan's corruption of the zodiac and see how it hides God's celestial plan for the earth. As we go through the star signs, we will begin to remove the veil that Satan has placed on the minds of unbelievers that they cannot see the glory of God.

With God's grace, we will also see that God has placed the revelation of the Gospel in the heavens so that everyone can gaze upon his plan of salvation and virtually read the Bible in the stars. However, just as the ink on the pages of the Bible are not 'the' Word of God but never-the-less convey the person and the message so that we can know him through it, so it is with the stars; they are inanimate bodies reflecting to us what God has revealed about himself.

We now know due to the Hubble Telescope and other space probes that there are other stars and galaxies not visible with the naked eye from the earth. This could cause some dispute or confusion unless we approach this from the point of view that God has so ordered the universe that its message regarding the Gospel is only clear from the perspective of standing on the earth. If we accept that God created the universe, then he placed each star and planet where he wanted. Therefore, we need to keep this in perspective as we unfold the twelve signs of the zodiac.

It is also worth noting that Satan does not relent in his corruption of heavenly things in order to deny God and hide the truth from man. Today the theosophical New Age Movement, especially GreenPeace; have taken the rainbow as one of their symbols. This icon is now powerfully corrupted. So much so, that if Christians were to adopt it into their ministry logo it would make them look like new age organisations. Unlike many Christians, the New Age Movement understands the significance of the rainbow as God's covenant with the earth through Noah after the flood.

As we contend with New Age spirituality, its corruption of Christian symbols, terminology and infiltration into the whole of society as well as in the Church, knowledge of Yahweh's Blood Covenants will become an important subject in our apologetics and evangelisation assisting us to turn people from worshipping the creature to the worship of its Creator. This will need to be the subject of another book in order to give it proper attention; however, a brief but precise explanation is in my book, 12 Steps to Divine Healing.

After the great flood recorded in Genesis chapter six and God's covenant with Noah and the earth, establishing the rainbow in the sky as his covenant sign in chapter nine, the descendants of Noah had become many nations and spread across the earth. Because they had the same origin, they all spoke the same language and could understand one another clearly. This was not only by virtue of a common language, but also because they were children of the covenant in union with God and by virtue of that possessed

36

the gift of understanding; it was not just a matter of understanding the words, but clearly grasping their full motivation comprehended in a clear manner. This was the case until some of them reached a valley called Shinar and settled there.

During their time in Shinar, they prospered greatly and became what we would call a civilization by virtue of using brick and mortar with which to build. The people were knowledgeable of the Mazzaroth and God's purposes set forth in it, and yet they became corrupt. With Nimrod as their king, they began to build a tower that would reach the heavens. "Come let us build a city and a tower with its top in the sky and so make a name for ourselves." *(Genesis 11:4)* A more accurate translation would be, "Let us build a tower with the heavens in its top." In other words, it was a religious planetarium containing a complete record and copy of the heavens expressed in an occult way. This is when the origins of the modern zodiacal astrology began; the names of false gods replaced the original names of the stars.

God noticed what they were doing and so he visited them to see what they had built. He then begins to taunt them. "If now, while speaking the same language, they have started to do this, nothing will stop them from doing whatever they presume to do. Let us go down and there confuse their language, so that one will not understand what the other says." *(Genesis 11:6-7)* God then confused their speech and scattered them all over the world. Because of this, we can find identical references to the zodiac in every culture across the world and they all relate back to this time in Babylon. This is also, why two people who speak the same language today often do not understand each other.

Nimrod's huge planetarium was an exact copy of the stars and the constellations and it was here that the origins of modern day astrology began and corrupted what God had originally shown in the Mazzaroth. It therefore denied Yahweh and made his creation a god in his place through which they could control their own destiny without God's interference; it became a means of hiding *(occult)*.

This was not the authentic use of astronomy or the Mazzaroth as God intended, but the occult use of the signs condemned in Deuteronomy and many other areas of scripture. Jim A. Cornwell says that the development of astronomy came from Babylonia around 1400-1000 BC with the Ea-Anu-Enlil tablets later followed by the records of celestial events and algebraic tablets of celestial motions.

The zodiac of Babylonia evolved around 420 BC before Berosos, Kidninu, Naburiannu and the Seleucid Babylonians appeared. He says that Ptolemy and Babylonia influenced the Arabs and India, which led to the term *manazil*. "Manazil" is an Arabic expression derived from an ancient Akkadian word that literally means "Mansion." Astronomy in Europe began around 600 to 300 BC with the pre-Socratic speculations, then Aristarchus *(Heliocentric theory)*, Eratostenes, Hipparchus and Ptolemy. Regarding the Lunar Mansions, the Arabs called them "Manazil al-Qama" and they use the Crescent Moon as the symbol for their religion and lunar calendar today that pre dates the Christian and Islamic periods relating back to the Babylonian Moon God Sin their supreme deity.

Astrology was a capital crime for Israel. That is why it remains a serious sin to dabble with the zodiac in order to plan our destiny or see into the future rather than putting our faith in God's plan of redemption and his promises for our provision and welfare. *(Matthew 6: 25-34)*

Chapter 6

The problem with the Horoscope;
a personal experience

Before experiencing conversion many years ago, I relied heavily on the daily horoscope. My dependence was such that without an in-depth reading for each day my plans or their potential would not be realised. Even my relationships were governed by the character-analysis as well as what had been cast, boxing people in to handle them or even manipulate them in subtle ways for personal gain; if the person's star sign did not match, a relationship with them would not be a serious consideration. It would often mean avoiding them completely and a judgmental attitude disguised as freedom of choice developed. *(Proverbs 16:2)*

This obsession began in a small and seemingly innocuous way with the conviction that it was just for fun with bad forecasts rejected as superstition. However, good forecasts would be accepted and acted upon and eventually a horoscope book was carried everywhere.

Not content or secure reading the daily horoscope analysis, reading what the newspapers and magazines had to say became a way of checking just to be sure, and over time, the whole thing became bondage. It was so absorbing that decisions made without consulting a star guidebook were rare.

One day, when speaking to a journalist, the subject of the horoscope came up. Shocked to discover he did not believe the horoscope, or even know much about it, he revealed that he was the one who wrote it in the newspaper that I read each day. He confessed that he often made it up to fulfil his obligations. Later, discovering that statistics showed publications that do not have a horoscope do not sell well was a surprise. That is why all major publications have one. This also reaches as far as magazine-style television shows that also have a horoscope segment.

Many people who read their forecasts will say they do not really believe in them. This of course is not true judging by the use of them in publications. If it were true, they would not dabble and there would be no demand for them as a priority for sales, and further to this, consulting an astrologist has become a major growth industry in recent years.

The telltale sign of having faith and belief in the horoscope is that people will reject a negative forecast but accept one that suits them. They can justify this by saying that it is only a bit of fun and they do not really believe in it. However, they give it credence when they even tacitly accept the possibility that a good forecast might be true for them.

When they do this, they accept a false god. In doing so, they sin by putting their faith in the horoscope *(or should we say horror-scope)* rather than in God's divinely revealed plan for their lives. *(Ephesians 1:3-23)* As John Sandford once said, *"Sin is taking by force what God would give by grace."* When we seek the future in this way or by divination, tarot card reading, fortune telling, palm reading, tealeaf readings, and such things, we are taking by force what God has promised by grace through his Word regarding his plan for our future. *(Ephesians 1:9-10, Ephesians 2:10)*

After becoming Catholic it was a shock to discover how many parishioners used the horoscope, divination and many other superstitious practices, not the least of which is the malocchio, *evil eye*.

One day after Mass, a group of friends gathered at our home for breakfast. One of the guests, a close friend was getting married and a discussion ensued about this.

One of the women asked for his partner's engagement ring. She put it on a length of cotton and held it in front of the girl. Looking deeply into her eyes they both concentrated on the dangling ring. Eventually the ring began to swing, a prediction and a conclusion followed about their future relationship. The direction of the first movement of the ring related to either the man or the woman, whichever being first received a prediction.

Familiar with such divinations before conversion, I knew that divination and fortune telling had no place in Catholic faith and belief and a polite explanation that God had a plan for our lives and that it was sinful to seek the future in any other way brought a patronising response. Everyone made light of the event and she continued doing the same with the other guests who delighted in the occasion.

At a charismatic conference some years ago, the speaker, a priest, said that many people that consult him regarding their problems tell him that their use of the horoscope and Ouiji Boards is only a game. He told the conference delegates, "For you it might be a game. But for Satan, they are his tools."

Reading the horoscope and using other superstitious practices is perverted faith. In fact, it is not faith at all but fate and it takes our focus from God and directs us to the creature if not Satan himself. This is exactly what the serpent did in the Garden of Eden when he diverted Eve's attention from the tree of life and focused it on the tree of the knowledge of good and evil. She did not hate God but forgot about him, and this is the same ruse of Satan today.

For those who take these matters lightly in these days of New Age enlightenment and pagan revivals of all things that worship nature and the creature, they should take God's views very seriously and repent. God has not changed the way he works nor has he relented of his hatred for this satanic corruption of his *(cosmic)* creation; a creation meant to reveal his glory rather than the creature glorying in the creation and thereby rejecting its Creator. In these days, people have even reviled heavenly beings *(God's holy angels)* by giving their names to deceiving spirits just as Nimrod did with the Mazzaroth in Babylon.

Because the occult zodiac hides the plan of God and denies Jesus, he condemns it in the most vehement way. In Isaiah 47: 9-15 he says, "Both these things shall come upon you suddenly, in a single day: Complete bereavement and widowhood shall come upon you for your many sorceries and the great number of your spells; Because you felt secure in your wickedness, and said, 'No one sees me.' Your wisdom and your knowledge led you astray, and you said to yourself, 'I, and no one else!' But upon you shall come evil you will not know how to predict; Disaster shall befall you, which you cannot allay. Suddenly there shall come upon you that you will not expect.

Keep up now your spells and much sorcery. Perhaps you can make them avail. Perhaps you can strike terror! You wearied yourself with many consultations, at which you toiled from your youth; Let the astrologers stand forth to save you, the stargazers who forecast at the new moon what would happen to you. Lo they are like stubble, fire consumes them; they cannot save themselves from the spreading flames. This is no warming ember, no fire to sit before, thus do your wizards serve you with whom you have toiled from your youth; each wanders his own way, with none to save you." In other words, God hates the horoscope and warns of his wrath towards those who do not repent and put their faith in him instead.

Revelations 21:8 regarding God's plan for a New Heaven and a New Earth reiterates this, saying that those practicing these deceitful things will not enter the Heavenly Jerusalem. The Catechism of the Catholic Church also makes this clear.

2116 All forms of divination are to be rejected: recourse to Satan or demons, conjuring up the dead *(channeling)* or other practices falsely supposed to "unveil" the future. Consulting horoscopes, astrology, palm reading, interpretation of omens and lots, the phenomena of clairvoyance, and recourse to mediums all conceal a desire for power over time, history, and, in the last analysis, other human beings, as well as a wish to conciliate hidden powers. They contradict the honour, respect, and loving fear that we owe to God alone.

2117 - All practices of magic or sorcery, by which one attempts to tame occult powers, to place them at one's service and have a supernatural power over others – even if this were for the sake of restoring their health – are gravely contrary to the virtue of religion. Wearing charms is also reprehensible. Spiritism often implies divination or magical practices; the Church for her part warns the faithful against it.

"So with us; when we were children, we were slaves to the elemental spirits of the universe. *(Galatians 4:3)* "See to it that no one makes a prey of you by philosophy and empty deceit, according to human tradition, according to the elemental spirits of the universe, and not according to Christ." *(Colossians 2:8)* "If with Christ you have died to the elemental spirits of the universe, why do you live as if you

43

still belong to the world?" *(Colossians 2:20)* "He reflects the glory of God and bears the very stamp of his nature, upholding the universe by his word and power." *(Hebrews 1:3)*

Chapter 7

How to calculate the times and dates of the celestial calendars

hen we look at the night sky, it is difficult to see the images ascribed to the constellation in the star charts. This is because the constellations do not really look like the names given to them. However, it is interesting to note that the names and expressions given to them are the same in every culture and language and they all go back to the same common root that was before the satanic corruption at Babel.

Independent of the name given to it, there are expressions referring to the zodiac in every culture, language and country on the earth. For example, the choice of a Dalai Lama is by the use of the horoscope. The Chinese, Chaldeans, and Egyptians have records involving the zodiac dating back more than 2000 years BC. In the temples of Bendera and Ezmay in the Egyptian background, they date back as much as 4,000 years BC.

Dr. Chuck Missler, former Branch Chief of the Department of Guided Missiles US Air Force, tells us that because of the way they are recorded, these records were drawn when the summer solstice was in Leo and presently in Aries and it moves about 1 degree every 71 years. He says that if we take the equator of the earth, imagine stars printed on a sphere as relative to the equator of the earth, and extend it outwards, we could draw a line on that celestial sphere, and that would be the celestial equator. The sun circumscribes an arc through the celestial sphere that is something other than following the equator.

Scientists still refer to the apparent path of the sun throughout the year called the ecliptic. Divided into twelve sections or signs with each sign consisting of three constellations, the path of the sun is 16 degrees wide. Due to the ancient and cultural references to these stars, by virtue of their positions in the imaginary figures, legitimate scientists interested in astronomy still reference the stars by their apparent positions in these constellations.

The ecliptic is like an angle in the sky and when it crosses the celestial equator it is called the equinox. There are summer and winter solstices as well as a spring and autumn equinox. The spring equinox is the arbitrary reference point for all mathematics in the celestial sphere. A celestial navigator as being the first point in Aries, which is just as the earth rotates on its axis and revolves around the sun, is also recessing because the angle of the spin of the earth is at an angle that is wobbling. In order to correct our calendar back to the ciberial calendar so we can get an accurate assessment of recorded time in the Old Testament, we have to add one day every four years and add one day every 25,579 years due to the wobble.

Because of the equinox when the days and nights are of equal length, which is when the sun is crossing the celestial equator, the equinox point itself is moving through the apparent heavens which move about 1 degree every 71 years. Chuck Missler says we know the dates of these ancient charts because we can roughly date them because of what they saw due to that procession. That is how we can infer that some of these records go as far back as 4,000 to 5,000 years by the ancient records of the constellations.

The Persians and the Arabians have traditions in their ancient history that the whole system called the astronomical nomenclature began with Adam, Seth and Enoch. This in not recorded in the Bible but they are testifying to it from what they could see in the stars. What is interesting about this is that the constellations they were studying already pointed to God in spite of the corruption. Josephus records that it began with Seth as a tradition and that Enoch actually preaches on the two judgments in that area on the fire and water regarding this.

Chapter 8

The truth behind the Zodiac

We will now take a brief look at each sign of the zodiac and see if we can discover God's redemptive plan hidden behind them revealed in the names given to the stars and constellations. With the help of Dr. Chuck Missler's *A Testimony to the Stars*, the in-depth research of Jim A. Cornwell, E.W Buller's *The Witness of the Stars* and my own research, we will discover what God has placed there, tearing down the veil that Satan has woven to cover God's purpose. By this, we will find God's revelation about Jesus written both in the Bible and in the constellations.

For the sake of brevity on this huge subject and since this book is about faith rather than astrology, Bible chapters and verses are included in preference to writing every scripture passage in full, so it will be important for you to read them in your Bible to get a fuller picture for further study.

As we take a short but precise journey through the celestial calendars, keep in mind that this book is not promoting the zodiac. On the contrary, the intention is to expose it for the lie that it really is and to restore the glory of God in his creation. By removing the veil of corruption, our faith in the Word of God will grow and we will understand it better experiencing the results God intended for us as a plan for the fullness of time to sum up all things in Christ in heaven and on earth. *(Ephesians 1:9-10)*

1: Unveiling the constellation of Virgo

Of all the constellations, Virgo is the most revealing regarding the birth, suffering, and death of Jesus. In Malachi 3:20 we read, "But for you who fear my name, there will arise the sun of justice with its healing rays" and as we have noted in chapter four, refers to the coming messiah.

The sun spends more time in Virgo than in any other constellation of the zodiac, entering on September 21 and not leaving until November 1. The sun is therefore within its boundaries at the time of the autumnal equinox, about September 23. The astrological period of Virgo begins in mid-August, which is when the sun entered the constellation 2,500 years ago *(500 B.C.)* when the Babylonians and Greeks created their version of the zodiac.

The Latin word Virgo literally means, *The Virgin*. The Hebrew name for the Latin Virgo is, Bethulah *(bthuwlah)* which is the Hebrew word used in Isaiah 7:14 where it says, "Therefore the Lord himself will give you this *sign*: the *virgin* shall be with child, and bear a son, and shall name him Immanuel."

Notice it says, 'the virgin' and not, 'a virgin' as referring to just anyone, but refers to a specific individual. Before this, we read that God is adamant in Ahaz demanding a *sign*. "And again the Lord spoke to Ahaz: Ask for a *sign* from the Lord, your God; let it be deep as the netherworld, or high as the sky!" In this context, this is clearly referring to the virgin birth. God gives the sign himself, which is to come from the House of David.

The virgin that shall conceive is the woman in Revelation 12, which started with Eve in Genesis 3:5. "I will put enmity between you and the woman, and between your seed *(offspring)* and hers." The seed of the woman shall come forth. The virgin refers to Mary and Immanuel *(Jesus)* because she is from the line of David. We also note that it mentions the word 'sky'. We read in Revelations 12 that a great *sign* appeared in the *sky*. This *sign* was a woman clothed with the *sun* that we know to be the Virgin Mary pregnant with Jesus our Immanuel.

When we look deeper into Virgo (Latin) and the constellations, there are brighter and lesser stars. This goes from the first brightest or first magnitude, getting fainter to the lesser magnitude. In Latin, the brightest star in Virgo called *Spica* means *a seed of wheat or barley*. In Hebrew, the star called *Thera* means *the seed*.

The word *seed* appears on two occasions in Genesis relating to Eve and the enmity between *her seed* and that of the serpent referring to God's war against Satan, and *Abraham's seed* relating to Jesus. The parallel to this is in Revelations 12:1-7.

The second brightest star in Virgo called *Tsemech* in Hebrew means *the branch* or *the shoot*. There are twenty words in Hebrew that can mean the branch; one of them is Tsemech. This is the only Hebrew word used exclusively in the Old Testament relating to the messiah and it appears in Isaiah 4:3, Jeremiah 23:5, Jeremiah 33:15, Zechariah 3:8, and Zechariah 6:12. All relate to Jesus, the coming messiah. The Arabic name *Al Zimach*, means *the branch*. In Virgos' hand is a branch, upon which is a smaller star called *Sibilon*, which means, *Branch*. (Zechariah 3:8; Zechariah 6:12; Jeremiah 23:5)

So far, in Virgo, we have *the virgin*, the seed, and *the branch*. In the ancient Greek star charts, we find a picture of Virgo with a tuft of wheat in one hand and a branch in the other. The Latin word *Spica,* which we have discovered, means '*a seed*' and it refers to the seed of wheat. It would seem that in the original scenario you could recount God's redemptive plan by reading the meaning of the names of the stars. (Romans 1:19-20)

In Virgo, we find another constellation called *Semchar* in Hebrew. The Egyptian star charts showed the original picture of this constellation as a woman sitting on a chair with a small boy standing on her lap. The Star of Bethlehem appeared in this constellation; the ancient Egyptian word for this is *Ches-nu,* which means, *the desired son.* In Haggai 2:7, we find the same expression as called *the desire of nations* that refers directly to Jesus. The star positioned above the baby called *Coma,* means, *desire of nations.*

Albumazar *(or Abu Masher)* an Arabian astronomer of the eighth century says that there arises in the first decan of the Persians, Chaldeans, Egyptians, the two HERMES and ASCALIUS that teach, *a young woman* whose Persian name denotes a pure virgin as sitting on a throne *nourishing an infant boy...* Having a Hebrew name by some nations called IHESU with the signification IEZA that in Greek is CHRISTOS. *(A Latin translation of his work is in the British Museum Library)*

The constellations are called *decans.* The word means *a part,* and used of the three parts into which each sign divides, each occupied by a constellation.

There is another constellation in Virgo called *Centaurus* and this Greek word means *man horse* with the concept of two natures. The Arabic and Chaldaic name for that constellation is *Beza,* which means *the despised one.* In Isaiah, 53:3 Jesus is the *despised of nations.* When Jesus was born, he was of two natures, God, and man. He was in fact, despised unto death.

There is a third figure depicted in the ancient charts of Virgo called *Bootes* and this means, *the exalted shepherd and harvester.* Isaiah prophesies, "He shall feed his flock like a shepherd: he shall gather the lambs with his arm, and carry them in his bosom, and shall gently lead those who are with

51

young.' *(Isaiah 40:11)* Jesus says of himself, "I am the good shepherd and I know my sheep and they know me." *(John 1:26-27)* Saint Peter refers to Jesus as the, "shepherd and bishop *(guardian)* of your souls." *(1Peter 2:25)* One of the stars in *Bootes* is, *Acturus*, which means, *watcher* or *guardian*. The *Bo* in Bootes means *the coming one*. John the Baptist said, "I am not the Messiah, but there is one coming after me and he is greater than me." *(John 1:26-27; Job 19:25)*

The constellation of *Beza* is adjacent to another constellation that is visible only from the southern hemisphere called, *The Southern Cross*. The former gold-mining town of Southern Cross in South Western Australia is a wheat-farming district and the main street is Spica Street. On a clear night, the Southern Cross constellation is so huge it seems to take up the whole sky. It is from here that this constellation is most clearly visible and hence the name of the town and its main street, Spica, *the seed of wheat.*

The ancient Egyptian Zodiac of Denderah depicts this constellation as a lion with his head turning back and his tongue hanging out as if thirsty. Jesus is the Lion of the Tribe of Judah and on the cross Jesus said, "I thirst."

Is it therefore a mere, or even a remarkable coincidence that in the one constellation called *The Virgin* we find the seed, the branch, the desire of nations, the two natures and the cross. It would be highly likely that the reason for the devil corrupting it at Babel was in order to cover it up and hide what God had written in the stars by replacing it with the names of pagan deities.

2: Unveiling the constellation of Libra

The constellation of Libra, as well as the rest, is no less revealing. The Hebrew name for Libra is *Mozanaim*, which means, *the balances* or *the scales*. The Arabic word for Libra is

Al Zebinah, which means *a purchase*. The Greek word for Libra is *Agora*, meaning *redemption*.

In Isaiah 40: 10-12 we read, "Here comes with power the Lord God, who rules by his strong arm; here is his reward with him, his recompense before him. Like a shepherd, he feeds his flock; in his arms, he gathers the lambs, carrying them in his bosom the ewes with care. Who cupped in his hand the waters of the sea, and marked off the heavens with a span? Who has held in a measure the dust of the earth, weighed the mountains in scales and the hills in a balance." In this text, we see both the redemption in verse ten, and the balances, scales and the measure in verse twelve.

The two stars in Libra are the Arabic words, *zuben al genubi*, which means *the price is sufficient*, or *zuben al shemali*, meaning *the price that covers*. The Hebrew name is *Kephar*, which means, *atonement: the price that covers*. In addition, in Libra, we find another constellation called *Corona Borealis*, which means, *the crown. (See Hebrews 2:9 and Zechariah 6:11-12) Sura* was one of the names used by the ancient Egyptians for this constellation, which means, *the lamb that has a crown*, a royal crown as the Hebrews called it. The brightest star called *Al Phecca* means, *the shining*.

At the crucifixion, we know that Jesus had a crown of thorns forced upon his head. The crown of thorns is associated with the price of our redemption revealed in this constellation called, *the balances*. Jesus' act of redemption balanced out the fall of Adam and the work of Satan and brought us into reconciliation with God by his blood that covers and redeems. *(Ephesians 1:7-10)*

The coming of the Messiah is the central theme of Ezekiel that relates to apostasy and a need for redemption. Isaiah prophesied the coming fall of Judea and the concept of salvation. *Scales and balances* from the Bible used as instruments for weighing are referred to in Isaiah 40:12 and Proverbs 16:11, as balance. Job 6:1-2 "...my calamity laid in the *balances* together!"

MENE, TEKEL, PERES are Aramaic words that suddenly appear on the wall of Belteshazzar's banquet hall *(Daniel 5:10)* which Daniel interpreted. Daniel 5:24-30 says, "This is the writing that was inscribed, MENE, TEKEL and PERES. These words mean: MENE; God has numbered your kingdom, and finished it; TEKEL, you are *weighed in the balances*, and are found wanting; PERES, your kingdom is divided, and given to the Medes and Persians." The New Testament Greek word for scales or balance is *Zugos* a yoke, a pair of scales as used in Revelations 6:5.

3: Unveiling the constellation of Scorpio

The Hebrew word for Scorpio is *Akrab*, which means, *the conflict* - see Psalm 114:1 that refers to training for war. The ancient Samarians called it, *the lawless one*. The whole of 2Thessalonians 2*ff* is about *the lawless one (antichrist)* and what is restraining him. In the ancient star charts, there are symbols in Scorpio depicting a strong man restraining a serpent while his feet are crushing the scorpion. The man's name derived from the Hebrew and Arabic version of the name *Afeichus* means, *the serpent held.* The brightest star is in the man's head called in Arabic, *Ras Al Hagus* meaning *the head of him who holds.*

The Arabic and Syriac groups knew this constellation as *Al Akrab*, which means *scorpion*, but it also means *the conflict*, or *war*. Syriac is an ancient Aramaic language 3rd to 13th century of several Eastern Christian churches. *Akrabbim (Hebrew. 'aqrabbim, scorpions)* a word always found with *ma'aleh*, meaning *the going up to, ascent of,* or *pass.* Therefore, *Scorpion Pass* is that near the southwest corner of the Dead Sea, the scene of Judas Maccabeus' victory over the Edomites.

The names of the stars on the heels *(Genesis 3:15)* are, *Dokar*, which means, *to crush* and *Shoef* that means *to bruise*. The brightest star is *Antares*, which means, *the accursed*. The man called Hercules in this constellation is kneeling on one knee with one foot on the head of Draco *the dragon. (Psalm 19:13; Matthew 28:18)* He holds a club in his right hand and his left hand holds a three-headed monster called Cerberus.

The brightest star called *Ras Al Gethi* means, *the head of him who bruises*. Revelations 20:23, tells us that when Jesus returns he will crush the antichrist, the lawless one, but Satan he restrains for a thousand years after which he is released for a short time.

It is very interesting to note that even in the zodiacal corruption at Babel, we still have this rendering of the antichrist crushed and Satan restrained. No matter how much the devil wanted to hide what God had established he simply did not have the power to eradicate it from the heavens. He could not reorder the universe to suit himself and therefore he opted for veiling it from us and confusing it in order to hide God's plan; a plan related to him and his ultimate defeat and so it is no wonder he is afraid of man and can only defend himself with lies, deceit and corruption.

4: Unveiling the constellation of Sagittarius

The Hebrew word for Sagittarius is *Keshef* and it means *archer*. This is also another centaur, *the double-natured one triumphing as a warrior*. The ancient Akkadian name for this constellation is *Nun-ki*, which means, *prince of the earth*. The brightest star in Hebrew is *Nai* meaning, *the gracious one*. Revelations 6:2, says, "I looked, and there was a white horse, and its rider had a bow. He was given a crown, and he rode forth victorious to further his victories." Again in Psalm 45:5-6, it says, "In the cause of truth and justice may your right hand show your wondrous deeds. Your arrows are sharp; peoples cower at your feet; the king's enemies will loose heart."

One of the stars in this constellation *Nashista*, means *going forth*. Nearby there are two other stars, one is *Nesher*, which means *the eagle*. The eagle is the traditional enemy of the serpent in both nature and Bible symbolism, and the other star is, *Norsar*, which means, *harp*, or *lyre*. The harp symbolizes the praises toward the one who triumphs. *Vega* is the brightest star, which means, *he shall be exalted*. The word *Lyra* means, *he gladdens the heavens*.

The object of all this is *Tunan*, which is the Hebrew word for *draco, the dragon, or the sea monster*. "On that day, The Lord will punish with his sword that is cruel, great, and strong, Leviathan the coiled serpent, and he will slay the dragon that is in the sea." *(Isaiah 27:1)* Draco depicted as a serpent falling is Greek which means, *trodden on*. The main star in this is *Al Waid*, which means, *he who is to be destroyed*. There is also a series of stars called *Ara*, which means, *he builds the fire of punishment*. This is a picture of an upside-down altar with its flame burning downwards. *(Revelation 20:9-10)*

5: Unveiling the constellation of Capricorn

The Hebrew word for Capricorn is *Gedi*, which means *a kid; a goat, kids of the goats of sacrifice* it also means *the cut-off* the meaning of atonement. The Arabic name for the star in this constellation is *Denab Al Gedi*, which means, *the sacrifice that comes*. *(Leviticus 9:3; 10:16)*

In the Old Testament, the kids of goats are a sacrifice on the Day of Atonement as a substitute for the people. They are *scapegoat* in Leviticus 16:15 and verses 20-28, and the priests would lay hands on the goat's head and speak into them the sins of the people. After which, the goat bearing all their sins is driven from the city to die.

God also provided a goat for Abraham's sacrifice in Genesis 22:13 that is a substitute for Isaac. Jesus called the *Scapegoat* and *the Lamb of God* is the sacrifice pleasing to God that pays the price of redemption as the *sin offering*. Sent out of the city bearing the sins of the world, Jesus is to die as our substitute. *(Isaiah 53:5)* Two major stars in Capricorn are *Gedi* and *Dabih*, which mean, *the cut off* and *the sacrifice slain*.

Capricorn depicted as a goat with its second half, as a fish tail appears to have fallen and awaiting death. The dolphin *(delhinus)* is the opposite of the eagle that is the constellation next to it where the eagle is falling, pierced and dying. The brightest star is *Al Tair*, which is Arabic for *wounding*. At the same time, its tail is full of life.

Ichtus, meaning *the fish* was the secret sign adopted by the early Christians and the sign of Ichtus drawn in the sand would confirm that they were talking of Christ. A fellow Christian seeing this sign would know the meaning behind it and thus acknowledge that they too were a believer. In fact, because they knew the true meaning behind the zodiac they could speak of Christ in zodiacal terms. It was a kind of open secret insomuch as their enemies would hear them speak and see the sign as that of the pagan zodiac and not as Christ and leave them undisturbed.

Delphinus means, *springing up again into abundant life.* This sign is symbolic of the Resurrection. To the ancient Chaldeans, this sign is *Rotanau*, which means, *swiftly running – as water flows*. The waters of baptism give us new life and resurrection. John in the river Jordan baptises Jesus who brings life to those who are perishing and later, Jesus commissions his disciples to baptise in water. Jesus also offers life-giving water. *(John 4:4-15; John 3:5; Revelations 22:1-5)*

6: Unveiling the constellation of Aquarius

Aquarius means *water bearer*. The Hebrew word for Aquarius is, *Dali*, which means *water bucket* found in Numbers 24:7 where it says that, "His wells *(buckets)* shall yield free-flowing waters."

When Jesus meets a Samaritan woman at Jacob's well, he asks her for a drink of water. The woman, surprised, asks where his *bucket* is because the well is deep. Jesus challenges her offering her living water from which she will never thirst again. Jesus needed neither a bucket nor a well because he is the bucket and the well from which the living water is flowing. *(John 4:4-15)*

This star sign is a man holding an urn, pouring an endless supply of water into the mouth of a fish called *Piscus Australis*, which means, *drinking in the heavenly flood*; the fish is drinking all the water poured out.

There are twelve signs of the Mazzaroth and there are twelve sons of Jacob. The sign of Judah is the Lion and there is a sign associated with each of the twelve tribes kept on a standard, *(a pole)* called an ensign. In Genesis 49ff, Jacob prophesies over each of them in order as he leans on his staff and takes them through the Mazzaroth. In so doing, the 'Dali' *(water bucket)* refers to Ruben, and Balaam refers to that in Numbers 24:17. In verse 17 it says, "A star shall advance from Jacob, and a staff shall rise from Israel." Biblical scholars associate the prophecy of Balaam with the Star of Bethlehem that heralds the birth of Jesus.

A 15th century historian records an account of Zoroaster who was a pupil of Daniel in Persia *(modern day Iran and ancient Babylon)* who interpreted dreams for king Nebuchadnezzar. The Zend Avesta - the Zoroastrian writings of that time, point out that when a new star appears in Virgo that it is very significant and a very important event. Zoroaster had said one thousand years after his birth, the priests *(magi)* will see a star in the sky and to follow it and they will come to a manger, and there they will find him. The corruption of Daniel's priesthood became Zoroasterism that includes the cabalistic sect known as the Magi. "The word magoi *(magi)* often has the meaning of "magician", in both Old and New Testaments *(Acts 8:9; 13:6, 8; also the Septuagint of Daniel 1:20; 2:2, 10, 27; 4:4; 5:7, 11, 15)*. The philosophy of the Magi, erroneous though it was, led them to the journey by which they were to find Christ. Magian astrology postulated a heavenly counterpart to complement man's earthly self and make up the complete human personality. His "double" *(the fravashi of the Parsi)* developed together with every good man until death united the two.

The sudden appearance of a new and brilliant star suggested to the Magi the birth of an important person. These three kings followed that star, found Jesus in the stable at Bethlehem, and worshipped him." *(Catholic Encyclopaedia)*

Water is used in two ways in scripture, the one is in John 3:5, says, "Amen, Amen, I say to you, no one can enter the Kingdom of God without being born of water and Spirit." See also Isaiah 33, Lord is rivers/streams; Joel 2: pours out the Spirit. Psalm 36:8-9 fountain of life. Jesus is the Living Water and Bread from Heaven.

7: Unveiling the constellation of Pisces

The Hebrew name for Pisces is *Dagon*, which means *fish* or *fishes*. Genesis 17:5-6, in some translations says, "His seed shall become a multitude of nations." Some biblical scholars maintain that this is a mistranslation and means, "Multiplying as the fish of the sea." This could be referring to the two sons of Joseph. *(Genesis 48:26)*

In the ancient star charts, there is a band between the two fish. The hoof that connects the two is the hoof of Aries the Ram. One fish is swimming towards the North Pole and the other to the sun. Although swimming in different directions the hoof of Aries, the band, connects them. Jesus, the Lamb, is the common bond and connection between the Old and New Covenants that, as the Alpha and Omega, completes them.

In 1Samuel chapter 5, we read about the Philistines, having captured the Ark of God, and transferred it from Ebenezer to Ashdod. They took the Ark of God and placed it next to their god Dagon only to find their god smashed to pieces the next day. *(1Samuel 5ff)*

8: Unveiling the constellation of Aries

Aries the Ram is the reference point for all the others. All the numbers go from the equinox that is in Aries. The Hebrew word for this is *Thalak* meaning *the lamb*. This Hebrew word is in 1Samuel 7:9, John 1:29, and Revelations 5:12. Each passage is referring to Jesus.

It is interesting to note that not only is Jesus the Alpha and the Omega as well as the Lamb of God but that Aries the Ram is also the central point of reference for all the other constellations from which all calculations are made - it is a kind of alpha and omega of the zodiac.

Jim Cornwell says that Aries, The Ram *(Middle English, zodiacal sign Aries, from Latin Aries, ram)* is on the meridian on December 10. The second smallest constellation of the zodiac is composed principally of only three lacklustre stars.

Aries is as a ram, an animal prized by the nomadic tribes of the Middle East. The zodiacal symbol represents the head and horns of the animal.

Around 4000 B.C. the sun was in this constellation on the winter solstice, which for some cultures marked the beginning of the year. By 1800 B.C. because of the apparent shifting of the sky due to precession, the sun came to be in Aries at the beginning of spring, which was true in Europe until the change from the Julian to the Gregorian calendar at the end of the 16th century.

Since the second century B.C., when the astronomer Hipparchus mapped the heavens, the vernal equinox and the point in the sky where the sun lies at that instant is referred to as *the first point of Aries*. The beginning of the astrological period called Aries coincides with the first day of spring, March 21, but because the precession of the equinoxes continues, the sun today is actually in Pisces at the beginning of spring and does not enter Aries until April 19.

Others call Aries *the lamb*, although it is a ram-like creature comparable to the Capricorn goat-like creature, giving rise to a fish. In the New Testament the Greek word for lamb is very similar to the word Aries, such as *Aren, ar-ane'*, a noun, the nominative case of which is found only in early times, occurs in Luke 10:3.

The astrological symbol shows the lamb facing backward with one paw on the band, which at one end holds the two fishes of Pisces, and the other end is bound to the neck of Cetus, the sea-monster, a varying picture of Satan, the great Leviathan of the Scripture. As in the first chapter of Job, God constrains Satan where he cannot do more than God allows him. Thus, Christ is with one hand upholding the Church and controlling and restraining Satan.

In the book of Revelation, we read that the power of Christ will chain Satan one day.

9: Unveiling the constellation of Taurus

Taurus is the Bull and the Hebrew word literally means *Bullock*. There are two horns on a bull regarded as the two sons of Joseph. The twelve signs of the Mazzaroth equate to the twelve tribes of Israel. However, there are in reality thirteen tribes. There are four camps of three tribes each. These make up the twelve tribes surrounding the Tabernacle that is in the middle. The Levites are the priesthood attending the Tabernacle. If removed to fulfil their ministry, there are only eleven tribes to take up the twelve positions.

This is resolved by breaking the tribe of Joseph into two tribes under Ethan and Manasseh who are the two sons of Joseph. Jacob has adopted Joseph's sons. When he gets to Egypt where we see Jacob and his twelve sons he has two sons from his gentile wife, these two sons are Ethan and Manasseh. In Genesis 38 Jacob crosses his hands and blesses the younger before the older but at the same time he is adopting them so there are actually thirteen tribes altogether.

In order to get the twelve tribes counting Levi you also count Joseph because he has a 'double portion'. However, if you leave the Levites out to take care of the tabernacle and count Ethan and Manasseh as two tribes, you still have twelve tribes surrounding the tabernacle. Taurus has two horns and in some renderings of the Mazzaroth, the chart speaks of the tribe of Joseph and the two horns being his two sons.

It is possible that in the corruption at Babel there comes the worship of the sacred bull. The Egyptian zodiac has the golden calf, which is a bull with the sun disk between the horns: the sun being in the house of Taurus at the time. We also find Isis, the virgin born saviour and through this, we can see that Satan does not miss a trick in his corruption.

Associated with Taurus, is a constellation called Orion mentioned in Job 38:31. Orion of course is the hunter whose Hebrew name is *chesnai*, which means *the strong one*. *Sieth* is the star meaning *Messiah*. *(Job 9:9. and 38:1 - Amos 5:8).*

There is another interesting constellation in Taurus called *Lepus*, which means, *the rabbit, the hare*. In the ancient star charts the word is used meaning *enemy* which makes sense when we realise the enemy is associated with *Ashtera* which is also know as *Eashtar* from which we have the pagan corruption called *Easter*.

This is associated with the Queen of Heaven whose worship included hot cross buns, eggs, and rabbits. *(Jeremiah 7:18. Jeremiah 34:15-30.)* Again, in the ancient star charts they show a river of fire that flows from Orion's foot that is crushing down on to the 'sea monster'. All this ties in with Isaiah 27:1, connecting the Messiah *(the strong man; Orion)* crushing the serpent. *(Daniel 7, Revelation 20:2-3, Psalm 53, Habakkuk 3:5, Isaiah30)*

10: Unveiling the constellation of Gemini

Gemini is *the twins*. In the Greek, it is two star groups; *Apollo* and *Hercules* and in the Latin, the names are *Castor* and *Polox*, the name of Saint Paul's ship in Acts 28:11.

Castor and Polox in Greek mythology are the two sons of Zeus who lived on Mount Olympus in the midst of the twelve gods of the Greeks. In maritime history, Castor and Polox have protected sailors from harm at sea. The more recent mariner term "By Jiminy" has its origin in calling on *Gemini* for protection.

The Hebrew name for Gemini is *Domun*, which means, *joined*. The Hebrews also called the constellation *Thaumin, the united*; the divine and human nature of the mission of Christ and used in the Old Testament in the sense of togetherness of persons *(Genesis 13:6)* fellowship *(Judges 19:6)* and praise *(Psalm 34:3)*. The Arabic name is *El henach*, which means, *wounded* or, *bruised* and *Mabushta* that means *tread under foot*.

From this, we can see the Righteous Judge and the Suffering Servant. It also makes sense of Saint Paul's debates with the Greeks on Mars Hill in Athens recorded in Acts 17:22-28 and we will look at this a little deeper in chapter eleven.

11: Unveiling the constellation of Cancer

This of course is the *crab*. The Hebrew names for the two stars that appear in Cancer are, *Solus Borius* and *Solus Australus*, which means the *Southern Ass*, and the *Northern Ass*. The ass idiom in Cancer connects to Ishachar in Genesis 49:11. The donkey or ass prophesied in Zechariah 9:9 is the symbol of the coming king of Jerusalem fulfilled in Matthew 21:5, referring to Jesus' entry into Jerusalem on Palm Sunday riding on a donkey.

Also found in Cancer is *Ursula Major* and *Ursula Minor* which is, *Big Bear* and *Little Bear, Big Dipper and Little Dipper*. Called *Greater Flock* and *Lesser Flock* they are the sheepfolds that are likely a reference to John 10:16. The Egyptian name for the constellation of Cancer is *Klaria*, meaning *the folds, the resting-places*. The seventh day of Cancer was God's day of rest. *(2Chronicles 6:39-42 - Isaiah 32:18)*

12: Unveiling the constellation of Leo

Leo is the Lion. The Hebrew word for lion is *Ah-ek* in Genesis 49:8-9. In the ancient charts, Leo is a lion leaping towards his prey, Hydra the sea serpent. Called *'The lion of the tribe of Judah'*, Jesus has the right to rule and judge the nations. In Genesis 49:10, it says, "The sceptre shall never depart." The right to rule also involves the right to dispense capital punishment.

When the Romans ruled Judea, the high priests in Jerusalem thought that the Word of God had been broken because the Romans had removed their right to administer capital punishment and because of this, they had no right to govern. That event caused the sceptre to depart from Judah. With reference to Genesis 49:10, they thought it had departed and that Shiloh had not come. Therefore, they put on sackcloth and ashes and wandered through the streets because the Word of God had been broken. However, unbeknown to them, at that time Jesus was already working in the carpenter's shop in Nazareth.

We see a connection between the Lamb of God that takes away the sin of the world, and the Lion of the tribe of Judah. Lion of Judah is a symbol of the tribe of Judah. John the Baptist announces Jesus, as the Lamb of God. Lambs are meek and Jesus came meekly and humbly to lay down his life as the Lamb of Sacrifice to shed his blood for the sins of the world. As the Lion of God, this represents his second coming when he shall come in great power and glory.

Leo is clearly a picture of the destruction of the wicked. *(Revelation 5:5)* Daniel described Babylon as a winged lion, a religious symbol used in the ancient pagan world while Peter warned his contemporaries that the devil prowls around like a roaring lion looking for someone to devour. *(1Peter 5:8)*

Chapter 9

The design and construction of the camp of Israel

*T*o cover all that we can know from references in the Bible to the constellations and God's plan would take a whole book in itself. However, this brief overview should give us some insight into what lay behind Hebrews 11:3 and give us something to work on as we look at the subject of faith and how it works for us as intended in Hebrews 11:2.

The interesting thing about the star signs is how the concept of God's plan recorded in the constellations is in the very substance of the Israelite's way of life throughout their history and it affected their whole society, life and faith.

They had specific rules of assembly when the tribes gathered around the Tent of Meeting and we find God's instructions for the Camp of Israel is in Numbers 2:2. "The Israelites are to camp around the Tent of Meeting some distance from it, each man under his standard with the banners *(ensigns)* of his family *(tribe)*."

At the centre of the camp was the Tabernacle with one door open to the East. The tribe of Levi has the priestly custody and care of the Tabernacle and so, they were in the centre. From the centre, there were three tribes to the north, three to the south, three to the West and three to the East. Because the Levitical Priests attended the Tabernacle, they are not lined up in this situation and so the tribe of Joseph divided into two by separating Ephraim and Manasseh resolves this as explained in the section on Taurus. To the east there are three tribes made up of Zebulon, Issachar, and Judah.

These were collectively known as, the tribe of Judah who rallied around the ensign of Judah. Zebulon's sign was Virgo: *Bethulah*, the virgin. Issachar's ensign was Cancer, the crab, and Judah's ensign was Leo, the lion. To the west, there is the tribe of Benjamin that includes Ephraim, Manasseh and Benjamin whose ensign is Taurus; the bull and Gemini; the twin. To the south, there is the tribe of Ruben made up of Simeon, Ruben, and Gad whose ensign is Aquarius: the water bearer *(man)*.

To the north, there is the tribe of Asher, Napthali and Dan whose ensign is Scorpio: the lawless one. This is consistent with that of the antichrist that is to come from the tribe of Dan. Not listed in the twelve tribes mentioned in Revelations 7 referring to the 144,000 sealed, it is conspicuous by its absence. Dan's sign is Cancer; Scorpion; however, the substitute for Dan is the eagle.

The sign for Napthali is Capricorn; the goat and Asher, Sagittarius; the bow. With the eagle as the substitute we have, the Lamb, the Archer, and the eagle. Which now leaves the *scales*: the *balances*: *the price is sufficient for redemption,* with Levi at the centre of the camp.

Around the Camp of Israel, there are now four ensigns: eagle, lion, calf, and man. These are the four faces of the cherubim at the throne in Revelation 4:5, so the Camp of Israel is a model of Heaven. These are the ensigns of the four Gospels about Jesus. He is the glory that manifest at the Tabernacle in the Holy of Holies. The Tabernacle contained the Law and Jesus is the one that fulfils it.

Looking at the camp from above, we will see that it is a cross with the Altar of Sacrifice and the Holy of Holies in the centre. In the design of a traditional Christian Cathedral, we will see the same design. The entrance to the Cathedral finds the font at the foot of the cross through which we must be baptised before entry for we too must come to the foot of the Cross and receive Jesus to ensure salvation. Along the central isle, the vertical beam, we come to the sanctuary and the high altar where the sacrifice of the Mass is celebrated on the centre of the two beams.

Behind the altar on the far wall is the bishop's throne where the sign nailed by Pontius Pilate on Calvary's cross declared him as King of the Jews. Two side altars in parallel to the high altar make up the crossbeam. The design of a Cathedral is that of a cross and the high altar is the sacrifice of Christ on Calvary celebrated at every Mass.

The centre is Christ and the order of the Mass is that the liturgy of the Word comes first, and then the liturgy of the Eucharist and so a Christian Cathedral is a model of heaven with Jesus as High Priest in the order of Melchizedech at the centre. We also note that in the following description of the four Gospels, it too forms a cross.

Chapter 10

The four Gospels and their Ensigns

The four Gospels are also a reflection of the camp of Israel; the eagle, the lion, the calf and the man and sometimes we see these symbols on a crucifix. Each symbol testifies to the mission of the four writers, Matthew - *man*, Mark - *lion*, Luke – *ox or calf* and John - *eagle*.

Symbolized by a man to represent the human nature of Christ, Matthew begins his genealogy from Abraham. A lion to represent Christ as king symbolizes Mark who has John the Baptist preaching "like a lion roaring" at the beginning of his gospel. An ox or calf to represent Christ as sacrifice and as priest, or to represent God's power symbolizes Luke who is also the author of the Acts of the Apostles. This also represents Mary as obedient, like an ox, as this is the only gospel where she says something. In addition, Luke's gospel starts on the duties of Zacharias in the temple. John's gospel represents Christ as God *(Logos)* or God's "all-seeing eye." Having a more developed theology, John's gospel records much that the other three synoptic gospels do not contain and it is the only gospel that does not have a genealogy in it, and so separate from the other terrestrial symbols, John's gospel is the eagle.

The word Genesis means; personified pre-existence and that is exactly where John's Gospel begins. Because the Gospels contain Jesus, the Word of God, they too are as a tabernacle and a promise of heaven when we accept by faith the truth that they contain for God and his Word is the same.

The Mazzaroth and its reflection in the camp of Israel gives us an outline of what could have gone on at the tower of Babel that was not just a pile bricks to touch the clouds but rather a serious affront to God's creation that expresses his divine plans for man. It certainly makes sense when we piece it all together to see what lies behind the occult and corrupt zodiac.

We can see why Satan has blinded the eyes of unbelievers so they cannot see the truth of the Gospel as Saint Paul says in 2Corintinas 4:4 because he has focused their eyes on the creature and the universe, rather than the creator. It also helps us to see why using the zodiac and a horoscope is a mortal sin considered a capital crime in Israel.

"And the Lord directed me at that time to teach you the decrees and laws you are to follow in the land that you are crossing the Jordan to possess. You saw no form of any kind the day the Lord spoke to you at Horeb out of the fire. Therefore, watch yourselves very carefully so that you do not become corrupt and make for yourselves an idol or an image of any shape. Whether formed like a man or a women, or like an animal on earth or any kind of bird that flies in the air or like any creature that moves across the ground or any fish in the waters below.

And when you look up to the sky and see the sun, the moon and the stars, all the heavenly array, do not be enticed into bowing down to them and worshipping them and worshipping the things the Lord your God has apportioned to all the nations under heaven." *(Deuteronomy 4:14-19)*

We cannot underestimate the seriousness of sin involved with the horoscope. God has not changed his ways nor has he changed his laws expressed in his spoken Word, for God's Word is his law and the only reality that God recognises, as we shall examine later.

Considering that, the Mazzaroth is in the Bible even up to the end of the Book of Revelations, we can accept that the Christians reading the Letter to the Hebrews also knew this. It is also clear that Saint Paul also knew this when he argues for Jesus on Mars Hill to the Greeks whose philosophy, religion and cosmology he knew as we will see in the next chapter.

Chapter 11

Saint Paul on Mars Hill
quotes from 'The Divine Signs'

Eudoxus of Cnidus *(now Turkey)* born in 408BC and died in 355BC was a major Greek philosopher, astronomer, and mathematician who accepted Plato's ideas that the planets rotated around the earth on crystalline spheres. Eudoxus produced a major work called 'Themon ne Phenomena' from which the king of Macedonia around 270BC asked a poet named Euratus to render into poetry a work named, "The Divine Signs."

Euratus was a native of Tarsus in Cilicia where Saint Paul was born and Saint Paul actually quotes from that poem in his address on Mars Hill, "Then Paul stood up at the Areopagus and said: 'You Athenians, I see that in every respect you are religious. For as I walked around looking carefully at your shrines, I even discovered an altar inscribed, 'To an unknown God.' What therefore you unknowingly worship, I proclaim to you.

The God who made the world and all that is in it, the Lord of heaven and earth, does not dwell in sanctuaries made by human hands, nor do human hands serve him because he needs anything. Rather, it is he, who gives to everyone life and breath and everything. He made from one the whole human race to dwell on the entire surface of the earth, and he fixed the order of the seasons and the boundaries of their regions, so that people might seek God, even perhaps grope for him and find him, though indeed he is not far from any one of us. For 'In him we live, move, and have our being, 'as even some of *your poets* have said, 'for we too are his offspring.' " *(Acts 17: 22-28)* The Greeks on Mars Hill knew he was referring to Euratus' poem, 'The Divine Signs' and recognised references to the constellations.

It is reasonable to assume that Saint Paul would have been knowledgeable of the Mazzaroth and what lay behind it; he was an educated man of his race as well as a citizen of Rome, and the Greek culture as well as its language had a wide influence on the culture of the Roman Empire.

For example, as we have seen in Gemini, he would also have known the Greek mythology regarding the name of his boat, Castor and Polox being the sons of Zeus as well as the goddess Aphrodite as identified with Ashtereth, *(Astrate) the goddess of the Sidonians* recorded in 1Kings 11:5 in his own Jewish background. *Ashtereth* means *womb* and she, as the Greek Aphrodite was associated with fertility. In the Egyptian background, she is associated with the goddess Qadash as the "Lady of Heaven." Qadash thought to be the daughter of the Egyptian sun god Ra is said to be a consort of Chemosh, the god of the Moabites *(Numbers 21:29; Jeremiah. 48:7,13,46)* the worship of whom was introduced at Jerusalem by Solomon in 1Kings 11:7. Closely related to Jewish history, it is likely that Saint Paul also knew these connections.

The author of the Letter to the Hebrews would also have known about the Mazzaroth and its associations with the surrounding pagan religions in their various idioms, and therefore there was no need for elaboration in verse two of Hebrews 11. They would have all known the meaning exactly and why the author immediately offers the lives of the men and women in the Old Testament as obvious evidence for faith and what it can accomplish.

73

When it came to Abraham's example, they would have understood that when God told him to count the stars and so should his descendants be God was really saying not only to count them, but also name them and put them in their proper order and sequence if you can, and so shall your seed be.

Because of his knowledge of the Mazzaroth, Abraham could read God's plan, the Gospel of Salvation written in the stars that were relating to Jesus. Due to his faith in God's promises, God rewards Abraham's faith as an act of righteousness and God considered him a friend. *(Genesis 15:7)* Saint Paul comments on this in his Letter to the Galatians where he says, "Realise then it is those who have faith who are children of Abraham. Scripture, which saw *in advance* that God would justify the Gentiles by faith, *foretold the good news* to Abraham saying, 'Through you shall all nations be blessed.' Consequently, those who have faith are blessed along with Abraham who had faith." *(Galatians 3: 7-9)*

Now that we have a little background knowledge about the Word of God regarding the cosmos and its constellations, let us see what faith can accomplish for us - for even the heavens, declare the glory of God for all to see and we now know that the universe was created by the Word of God. We now know this, not by blind faith alone but due to the evidence before our very eyes.

It is significant that the plan of salvation written in the stars as we have looked at, are clear to see only from the earth because viewing the same constellations from another planet or position beyond the earth would change the order since the stars we see are not on a flat surface. From our view, one star next to another could be millions of light years away from each other receding into space. This means that the Gospel is for us on this earth and revealed in the things we see in the night sky; a sign of God's universal and unending love for us.

If God can order the whole creation by speaking his Word, then we should gain much courage from what that same Word can do for and in us, since in our days God's Word has been spoken in human form; Jesus Christ to whom all creation and history points as its Alpha and Omega. The Hebrews understood this and therefore, we too, can gain a deeper understanding so that our faith will grow according to it.

Chapter 12

Faith and the Old Testament; what it accomplished.

We can now move on to Hebrews 11: 4 and begin to discover what faith accomplished for those in Old Testament times as presented by the writer as examples. Obviously, Abel, Enoch, Noah, Abraham, Isaac, Jacob, Moses, Joshua, Rahab as well as the others that the author of Hebrews didn't have time to mention in chapter eleven such as Gideon, Barak, Samson, Jephthah, David, Samuel and the prophets, not only understood what faith is and how the universe began, but accomplished miraculous and impossible things by reason of it.

These were such amazing things as offering a greater sacrifice to God, accomplishing a bodily ascension into heaven without dying, having the knowledge of a global deluge before it happened and the ability to survive it. Inherit righteousness, gain the pleasure and friendship of God, have the power to extend your life beyond the normal time span and produce children from God when you are over ninety years old.

Know the future and God's plans, protect your children from destruction, have the ability to reject worldly power, influence, and riches to accept the greater wealth of God's anointing, have the courage to leave what you know and go to a place you do not know let alone how to get there and find it. Inherit great wealth by not asking for it, overcome fear, part a sea with a stick, and walk through it with dry feet with a whole nation of people following you safely. Bring down bread from heaven and get natural mineral water from a dry rock only using a stick or get better than Kentucky Fried Chicken free from heaven to feed a whole nation.

Perhaps you would like to cause great cities to crumble within seven days as you play a trumpet, discern what is from God and not perish with the disobedient even though you are a harlot, have the ability to make the world unworthy of you, and receive God's approval for it. Conquer entire kingdoms or close the mouths of lions without effort, put out raging fires without lifting a finger or calling 911, escape death, become powerful in spite of your obvious weakness, and become strong in battle. Easily turn back nasty invaders who would pillage you, receive the dead back to life, accept martyrdom with joy, and endure mockery, scourging, chains, and imprisonment.

If this is looking good maybe, you might like to get out of jail without a trial, smite giants who bully you and conquer a powerful army single handed at the same time with only a bit of leather and a pebble. Live in a furnace for a few days and not become singed by the faggots, have God send a fiery chariot to escort you home when your time comes, find heavy iron hammers that are lost in a river by causing them to float to the surface of the water. Cause the sun to wait a few days until you have finished what you have to do before it sets or get your enemies to give you all their money when you leave their country and not pay departure tax. Understand donkeys when they try to talk to you or cause God to give you an extra fifteen years to live after he said you would die and then get him to order the sun to travel backwards for ten steps just to prove it to you.

All this is only a portion of what faith can accomplish and God thinks it is just wonderful; it would be interesting to see scientific theories try that one, let alone explain it.

Looking at this list which doesn't even get close to the New Testament promises, it's no wonder the author did not have time to tell the Hebrews everything that faith can do. With a history and an unending list like that, Hebrews chapter eleven would still be in the process of completion in ever increasing volumes and we would never hear the rest of the story.

The amazing thing is that all the people spoken about in the Old Testament not only believed that those things were possible, but they believed them without any evidence and, actually accomplished them in spite of their frailty. No wonder God was pleased with them and why it says that without faith it is impossible to please God and that we must believe that he exists and that he rewards those who seek him. *(Hebrews 11: 6)*

Well, if we also want to please God, then we must learn what faith really is and how to apply it effectively in our lives enabling us to get the result that God and we desire. Clearly, faith is the active force needed in living as a powerful and fulfilled Christian. After all, Jesus tells us that we will do the works that he did and yet, do even greater ones. *(John 14:12)*

Considering that all those people mentioned are living and operating under an old covenant without the benefit of God teaching them though Jesus personally, then surely, we should be able to achieve even greater things through faith. Why is this so? Because our new covenant with better promises is more reliable: Jesus is the mediator of the new covenant and he always responded to faith just as his Father had done. *(1Timothy 2:5, Hebrews 8:6, Hebrews 9:15, Hebrews 12: 24)*

One has to wonder now if the short explanation to the Hebrews of what faith is, was more to do with faith in the listeners ability to grasp by faith what it didn't say about faith because they surely didn't get much evidence from what little the author said about it in that first verse. However, it at least explains more than Jesus did when asked about faith. Of course, Jesus had greater faith and that is probably why he said less to his disciples when they asked for an increase. This of course means that since I am writing a whole book on the subject it makes me wonder if I have any faith at all if I follow that line of thinking. Well, let us 'see'. As we read on, let us look to Jesus, the author and perfector of our faith because it is certain that by faith, your faith will grow. *(Hebrews 12:2)*

Chapter 13

Abraham's seed and the promise in the stars

What else did the Hebrews know from the statement, "By faith we understand that the universe was ordered by the Word of God, so that what is visible came into being through the invisible." Obviously, the writer did not need to elaborate on it before he spoke about what the great men and women of the Old Testament had done through faith.

If you are wondering why there is an elaboration of this one subject here, it is simply because the Letter to the Hebrews makes a point of it related to faith. It seems therefore expedient that we know this too if we are going to understand his teaching on faith and its cosmogony revealed in these three short verses of Hebrews 11: 1-3.

The cosmogony continues to unfold in Psalm 147:4 where it says, "He numbers all the stars, calls each of them by name." Again, in Isaiah 40:26 he says, "Lift up your eyes on high and see who created these: He leads out an army and numbers them, calling them by name. By his great might and strength and power not one of them is missing."

In other words, look up into the heavens and see who created them. The army is the stars and the constellations in the cosmos and God has counted each one and named all the stars placing them in their order and sequence and none is missing; God has placed them exactly where he wants them to show forth his purposes.

When God calls Abram to let him know that Ishmael will not be his heir but Isaac, his own issue will be his heir, he tells Abram to look up into the sky and count the stars if he can and so shall his descendants be. Abram put his faith in the Lord, who saw it as an act of righteousness; justified, Abram finds favour in God's eyes due to his faith and God immediately begins to cut a covenant with him and he becomes known as Abraham. God had taken the "H" from Yahweh and placed it in Abram's name and this covenant name exchange made Abraham the man of God and Yahweh the God of Abraham.

It is through this covenant that God will bring forth Isaac. Isaac is a type and foreshadowing of Jesus who fulfils the covenant some centuries later. *(Genesis 15:5-6)* When we take a deeper look into this text we discover that God is really asking Abram to not only count the stars but to name them in their proper order and sequence if he can and thus shall his *seed* be as we have previously noted.

The word *descendants* in the plural appears to be an error of translations or it could be referring to the physical genealogy up to Jesus who will have many brothers in an unending number who are those who are born again from above and who receive baptism. Jeremiah 34:22 records "Like the host of heaven which cannot be numbered, and the sands of the sea which cannot be counted, I will multiply the *descendants* of my servant David and the Levites who ministered to me."

Mary is of the line of David and it is from Mary that the Word *(the seed)* of God takes flesh and so this makes sense of the plural *descendants* regarding God's promise to Abraham. In Galatians 3:16, Saint Paul addresses the plural, "Now the promises were made to Abraham and to his descendant. It does not say, 'And to descendants', as referring to many, but as referring to one, 'And to your descendant,' who is Christ." The Hebrew word used is 'seed' that is singular.

When we compare Abraham in Genesis and Paul in Galatians regarding descendants, descendant and seed, there is no contradiction; one is referring to the physical genealogy and the other to faith. In verse eight, it says, "Scripture saw in advance that God would justify the Gentiles by faith, foretold the good news *(Gospel)* to Abraham saying, 'Through you shall all the nations be blessed.' Consequently, those who have faith are blessed along with Abraham who had faith."

Those blessed along with Abraham are human beings in the physical realm, born again from above by an "imperishable seed" that is the Word of God *(1Peter 1:23)* and so by faith in God's Word we are consequently brothers of Jesus in his humanity as well as adopted by his blood *(Ephesians 1:7-10)* and children of Abraham by faith. Made possible by faith in the *descendant* Jesus Christ, our humanity and our faith in the Word of God combine and bring forth a new creation and thus the divine image is complete and restored. *(2Corinthiams 5:17, Galatians 6:15)*

In other words, written in the stars Abraham could see the good news of Jesus Christ; the constellations are actually preaching the Gospel to Abraham in advance and Saint Paul is ratifying it to the Galatians who, along with all those who accept the *descendant* inherit the Kingdom of God by faith and by faith, they are children of Abraham. The whole of the Old Testament is a shadow of the New and it proclaims the Gospel.

Chapter 14

The Word of God and a Cosmology of Mary

"**N**ow the promises were made to Abraham and to his descendant. It does not say, 'And to descendants', as referring to many, but as referring to one, 'And to your descendant,' who is Christ." *(Galatians 3:16)* Regarding the descendant, it is difficult to grasp the action of the Incarnation and it remains a mystery in the full sense of absolute knowledge. However, it is possible for us to gain some insight by what God has revealed through the Bible. When the Archangel Gabriel appears to Mary, he tells her that the Holy Spirit will come upon her, and the power *(dynamis; miraculous power, ability, abundance, might, strength, mighty works)* of the Most High will overshadow her. *(Luke 1:35)*

The Holy Spirit did not infill Mary on this occasion but came upon and overshadowed her. This is in keeping with the action of the Holy Spirit throughout history until the day of Pentecost when he indwelt man permanently for the first time as "the Promise of the Father" that Jesus spoke about before his crucifixion. *(John 7:39)*

The power or the shadow of the Most High refers to the cloud that filled the Holy of Holies above the Ark of the Covenant. Inside the cloud was the shekinah glory of God. The word *glory* means, that which is impressive or influential about a person. The glory of God is what is impressive and influential concerning God. The word shekinah means *the divine presence* from the root word *shakhan* meaning *Habitation of God* and it refers to the Word.

God tells us in Revelation 21:3, "Behold, God's dwelling place is with the human race." Moreover, this is where God desires to be – with you. Only by the Logos and the Rhema becoming flesh could God do this. The Word filled Mary at the Annunciation; the very same Word that had created her flesh that was holding it in being. In some miraculous way, the Word so imbued what it had created and took that flesh upon itself; it became one.

The substance of the flesh even at a sub-atomic level, lives, moves, and has its being in the Word and so separation is not possible. In some way, the Incarnation was a fusion of these two agents of creation according as God willed it and Mary became the Ark of the New Covenant containing the Word: the personified pre-existing Christ who was with God in the beginning. Mary now becomes the new Eve who is to bring forth the new Adam thus restoring by obedience to the Word that which was lost in disobedience to it at the fall in Eden. Revealed at the marriage feast at Cana, we can see this event unfolding between Jesus and Mary and it will give us some insight to the relationship of Mary and the Word and her rightful place in God's plan as the Queen of Heaven and so we will look at that in more depth in the next chapter.

The action of the Word even upon and in our own flesh should not be such a problem for us to accept when we consider the action of the Word on mere bread and wine. We believe by the grace of faith that Jesus Christ is present, body, soul and divinity in the Eucharist and we know this happens at the Consecration when the priest speaks the words of Jesus, "This is my body... This is my blood." If we can believe the very substance of those species change by the spoken Word: the Rhema of God Incarnate, then it should not be too difficult to take the same faith and apply it to what the Word of God has to say about our lives, and what it can do in, and for us too. After all, these were not the only words that Jesus spoke.

Nor should it be a great problem to understand that the Word of God in us also becomes one, and where the Word is, there are we also. We know from baptism that if we have died in him, and thus risen along with him we can grasp some hint of our own resurrection. *(John 17:10-11; 20-24; Ephesians 1:4)* In addition, it should not be too difficult to see how the spoken Word of God brought the universe into existence from nothing because Psalm 33: 6 says, "By the Lord's *word* the heavens were made; by the breath of his mouth their entire host."

Saint Paul mentions Abraham who was righteous and justified because he believed God's promise. We too gain God's favour simply by taking God at his word by faith as Abraham did and thus we are elevated into heavenly places. *(Ephesians 2:6)* Jesus is very serious about the way we accept his word, he says, "Heaven and earth will pass away, but my words will not pass away." *(Matthew 24:35)* God's word is therefore eternal and existed before all things existed and will remain forever. For our immediate comfort, he tells us that if we build our house, that is, our lives on the Word of God it will not only stand strong and last forever but we will be able to weather the storms of daily life and considered wise by doing so. *(Matthew 7:24-27)*

As we unfold this cosmology of faith, it is not possible to leave Mary out of the picture for she plays a prominent role in God's salvation plan, most especially regarding the Incarnation of the Logos. Sadly, some Christians balk at the idea of the assumption of Mary into heaven because there is no record of it in Holy Scripture. However, there are many things not recorded in the New Testament and we know there were many letters as well as gospels that did not find a place. John's Gospel testifies to this at its conclusion, "There are also many things that Jesus did, but if these were to be described individually, I do not think that the whole world could contain the books that would be written." *(John 21:25.)*

In order to establish a case for the assumption of Mary into heaven in a simple way and for the sake of brevity, let us appeal to reason and logic in these very simple questions. Who is the greater, Elijah who did not see death but taken into heaven in a fiery chariot, or the Mother of Christ whose flesh contained the Logos? Who is greater, Enoch who did not see death but was simply seen no more, or Mary, the Mother of Christ whose womb contained the Son of God? Who is greater, those that did not give birth or give flesh and blood to the Incarnate Word of God, or Mary?

If you say Mary, then the question remaining would be, why then would God discard the very flesh and blood that gave human life to his only begotten Son and let it decay in the ground when those far less worthy did not see corruption? It is unreasonable and even illogical to think such a thing. Consequently, we must reason by faith that Mary, the Mother of Jesus was also taken into heaven as the first to experience salvation after the resurrection.

It is also worth noting in this regard that Jesus, conceived by the Holy Spirit did not have the flesh of both father and mother as we do; Jesus physical body came only from Mary.

It seems unthinkable therefore, that Jesus would use his mother as an incubator and discard it when it had completed its function. If the body and blood of Jesus Christ was holy, then also that of Mary from which it came for it was the only flesh and blood chosen by God before time began to give physical birth to the Logos. Blessed therefore is Mary amongst women and blessed above all creatures.

In Genesis 3:15-16, referring to the serpent, God says, "I will put enmity between you and the woman, and between your offspring and hers; he will strike at your head while you strike at his heel." Later in scripture and history, we find Isis, the virgin born saviour associated with the constellation of Taurus as we have looked at in chapter eight in which there is also a constellation called Lepus *the rabbit*, which means *enemy*.

The enemy is associated with *Ashtera*, which is also known as *Eashtar* from which we have the word 'Easter'. This is associated with the Queen of Heaven whose worship included hot cross buns, eggs, and rabbits. *(Jeremiah 7:18. Jeremiah 34:15-30.)* The ancient star charts show a river of fire that flows from Orion's foot crushing down on to the 'Sea Monster' found in Isaiah 27:1, connecting the messiah *(the strong man; Orion)* crushing the serpent. *(Daniel 7, Revelation 20:2-3, Psalm 53, Habakkuk 3:5 Isaiah 30)*

Although there is an explanation of this in the constellation of Taurus, it is worth noting again due to the title Queen of Heaven and the position of the New Eve, Mary has that place and title, thus overcoming Isis *(the goddess religions)* and defeating Satan's position in the heavens. It is no coincidence that this is also associated with Easter; the Resurrection of Jesus who through his cross and resurrection destroys Satan's rule and crushes the serpent's head. Mary therefore is, "a woman clothed with the sun, with the moon under her feet, and on her head a crown of twelve stars." The twelve stars are the tribes of Israel whose ensigns were those of the twelve constellations. Therefore thus restored, she rightly deserves the titles, Mother of God and Queen of Heaven. *(Revelations 12)*

Chapter 15

Mary restores Eve at Cana and reveals the New Adam

Saint John records the restoration for Eve's rebellion at the Wedding Feast at Cana in chapter two verses one to eleven. This is significant regarding the fall of Adam and Eve and the role of Jesus and Mary.

Other than the annunciation, the nativity and the finding in the temple we hear no more about Jesus until his Baptism in the Jordan when God reveals Jesus' mission and public ministry. From there, we begin to see the unfolding revelation of his glory at Cana.

It is significant that Jesus did no miracles after returning from the desert and when the Holy Spirit came upon him at the Jordan until the wedding feast at Cana. At Cana, the simple exchange between Mary, Jesus, and then the servants, concluded the Old Testament and became the catalytic beginning of the new and everlasting covenant and a time of grace; Eve had initiated the rebellion in Eden, Mary initiated the event at Cana, and it is significant that it was at a wedding feast.

This was something Mary had to do because Jesus was obedient to the fourth commandment that says, "Honour your father and your mother that all may go well with you and you have a long life upon the earth." Moreover, he would not rudely ignore his mother by suddenly overruling her and leaving for his mission.

Therefore, Mary initiates the process saying to Jesus, "They have no wine." In doing so, she was releasing Jesus from her maternal authority to cling to his bride, the Church; thus reflecting and fulfilling Genesis 2:23-24. In doing so, Mary was also repairing the damage caused by Eve in the Garden of Eden when she ignored her husband and listened to the serpent; Mary was now submitting to Jesus and revealing him as the Bridegroom and the New Adam. At the same time, she was revealing herself as the New Eve *(Revelations 12)* and Mother of the Church in submission to Christ as its head.

Until now, Jesus had been in submission to his mother obedient to the fourth commandment, but at Cana Mary was submitting to Jesus as the New Adam *(1Corinthians 15:45-49)* thus releasing him into ministry. *(Ephesians 6:1-4)* This exchange repaired the damage done in Eden and restored the proper roles of Adam and Eve ushering in a new age of grace through Jesus Christ as Lord. The significance of a wedding is important because it was a symbol and reflection of the wedding feast of the lamb in the book of Revelation.

At the wedding feast at Cana, the changing of water to wine not only reflected the water and the blood that gushed from Jesus' side on Calvary; a fulfilment of the water and blood sprinkled on the doorposts with a hyssop stick during the Passover in Exodus, but it also changed marriage from a mere contract into a sacrament. Just as a marriage is a blood covenant due to the hymen being broken and blood flowing that consummates the marriage, it is a reflection and a type of Jesus and the Church at the wedding feast of the Lamb and the consummation in heaven.

The idea of blood in a marriage and Adam's acclamation regarding Eve that said, "At last this is flesh of my flesh and bone of my bones" is present at Cana. What is in the centre of your bones? Is it not marrow? Marrow is where blood is made and the building block of the body and its health, and the body is 98% water. This was also reflecting the new covenant in the body and blood of Jesus on Calvary; the flesh also refers to the Eucharistic bread and the blood refers to the Eucharistic wine.

Again, this reflects the blood of the lambs and the water sprinkled from the hyssop stick onto the wooden doorposts at the Passover in Exodus and the blood and water on Calvary that flowed from Jesus side onto the wood of the cross as well as the water to wine at Cana. It was also the tradition of the time to add a little water to wine and this is what Jesus also did at the Last Supper when he instituted the Eucharist: the reception of which changes those who have faith in this miracle.

A memorial meal concluded the nine steps of a Hebrew Blood Covenant ritual only after which the participants can be known as friends. It is therefore significant that on the cross Jesus drinks the bitter wine offered to him on a hyssop stick that also contains water in its stem and says, "I thirst." After this he said, "It is finished!" and gave up his spirit and the new and everlasting covenant was now established.

For those that do not attend a Catholic Mass, it is worth noting that the priest puts a small amount of water into the wine before the consecration. The prayer accompanying the mixing is incarnational: "By the mystery of the water and wine, may we come to share the divinity of Christ who humbled himself to share our humanity." Through the Mass, the sacrifices of old are completed.

The teaching of Saint Paul about wives submitting to, or being subordinate to their husbands does not intend to demean women. Ephesians 5:22-24 "Wives should be subordinate to their husbands as to the Lord" and Colossians 3:18 "Wives, be subordinate to your husbands, as is proper in the Lord" did not mean being under the thumb as many men have treated women over the centuries. That idea seems to have ignored Ephesians 5:21 where it says "Be mutually subordinate to one another out of reverence to Christ."

Rather than being under the thumb, subordinate means, *arrayed under*. A woman fully arrayed in her femininity is vulnerable in her beauty, but under the protection of her husband, she is safe and free to be fully who and what she is without shame or fear.

In the days when the men would be away from home for many years, usually fighting battles only the women, young boys, girls, babies and the elderly would be left at home. In order to become unattractive to men the women would not wear perfumes or dress up; they would cover up their bodies as well as their faces so that roving males would not lust after them. When the news came that their men were coming home, the women would immediately wash, perfume and dress in their finest attire; they would array themselves for their husbands and await them.

Fully arrayed, a woman is irresistible to men and so it is necessary to ensure her safety, protection and security, and only the man can do this. When the husband arrived at his home he would enter, place his spear across the doorposts and locking the door behind him would go to his wife. The spear across the door told anyone that wanted to enter that they would die if they tried and therefore the woman was under his protection and free to array herself in all her beauty and feminine sensuality.

Adam however, did not protect his wife during the seduction by the serpent. By the authority that God had given him, he could have corrected the lying exaggerations of the serpent regarding the two trees but he did not do this;

91

he listened to his wife who did not defer to her husband who was with her at the time and he said nothing either to his wife or to the serpent.

Even though Eve took the fruit and ate of it, she did not die immediately. Adam seeing this accepted that God had lied as the serpent indicated and ate of the tree himself. Because God had given Adam the instruction and authority, he broke covenant with God when he did this. It was at this point that sin and death entered the human condition. As in the case of Eve, Adam did not die immediately. In fact, Adam lived for another 930 years before he expired physically. However, the process of death had entered Adam through his separation from God when he sinned and this is where our problems began and why all men die.

Man is an immortal being, not created to die. Created to live forever, the human soul and spirit cannot die and so spiritual death as a separation from God reaches its conclusion when a person's name, blotted from the Book of Life ceases to exist. When this happens, God views the person as never existing or created and blots them from his memory and as far as he is concerned, he had never thought of them.

For the person, not only is the memory intact but also there is a complete knowledge of who God is and what they have lost with no hope or solace. For that person eternal life is eternal death experienced without dying in the full knowledge of what eternal life with God could be. This is the second death and what the Bible calls hell. Therefore, death is both a separation of the body from the soul; the physical death that returns to dust, and the soul, separated from God for all eternity is the spiritual death, unless redeemed by Christ through faith while in the body.

Faith however, is the freely given gift of God through grace that saves us when we accept Jesus Christ and in doing so, we are born again. After our physical death, we receive a new incorruptible body at the resurrection.

When Adam partook of the fruit, Satan took legal control of the world and with it all the evil, disease, and filth of Satan's dark kingdom ushered in.

As the New Catechism of the Catholic Church states, "Sickness and disease came through sin in the first place." *(1505/440)* The serpent had succeeded in turning their faith away from what God had said in order to accept what he says, and this is still the nefarious distraction he uses today.

Because Adam and Eve suffer banishment and separation from God and along with them, all human generations, Mary's submission to her son at Cana restores Eve's disobedience and reflects Mary's new relationship to Jesus that is the example of the relationship of the Church in obedience to Christ as Head of the Body.

This is what Saint Paul also teaches regarding wives being subordinate to their husbands as the Church is to Christ. However to overcome Adam, Saint Paul tells the husband that he must love his wife as his own body and be prepared to die for her as Christ died for the Church. The Church therefore arrayed fully in submission to Christ is under his protection, thus the Church has the authority to act in his name. *(Ephesians 5: 21-32)*

The fact that this took place at a wedding feast also showed Mary's maternal concern for the bride and groom; they were no doubt friends of the family and because a Jewish wedding feast lasted for seven days, it would have been very embarrassing for the couple if the wine ran out before the completion of the feast. Mary's maternal concern caused her to mention it to Jesus and as a result, it also established her new role as the Mother of the Church under the headship of Christ; "They have no wine." When Jesus responded, "Woman, what has that to do with me? My hour has not yet come." Jesus was relating to the crucifixion being the hour.

The wedding lasted seven days, and seven is the number of completion in Biblical terms and it reflected the creation in Genesis. The three days *(John 2:1)* were referring to Jesus time in the tomb. The first three days of the wedding also represented the natural order and the next four days represented the supernatural completion.

The first wine, although a genuine wine, represented our limitations in natural terms. The water represented our human and limited ability and the best wine represented a new, eternal, supernatural life and ability given abundantly in Christ through whom we become a new creation. This brings us to completion able to enjoy the seventh day rest with God.

The intervention of Mary at the wedding revealed the supernatural provision of God that was the new wine reflected in the new covenant referring to the hour for which was still to come. It also revealed the new birth attained through the blood of Christ giving us new life by the Holy Spirit. It also reflected Saint Paul's teaching that when a person accepts Christ they become a new creation; the old has passed away and the new has come. *(2Corinthians 5:16-19)*

The water in the jars also represented the things in the natural, but the new wine, the best kept until last, was showing the transformation from death to life. The fact that it was water to wine was also significant because the water also represented our natural birth. Our natural birth takes place when the water breaks and the baby born.

The new wine represented our transforming new birth from above through the blood of Christ and the beginning of our new supernatural life; God can take what is tasteless, colourless, and limited in our own natural efforts and brings them to completion by supernatural grace. In fact, without this revelation, it is impossible in human terms; we get so far on our own efforts and before it is completed, we run out, as did the first wine.

These few words of Mary, *("Do as he tells you")* declared Jesus as Lord. When Jesus revealed the miracle of Cana, it was the tiny pinpoint fulfilment of the old and the pinpoint beginning the new; now Jesus could reveal his glory and the disciples saw it.

Cana was also revealing Mary as the new Eve and Jesus as the new Adam and the true vine *(John 15)* replacing the false vine and the bitter wine of affliction in Genesis 3:1-7. By faith, we are the branches that produce fruit when we abide in the Word. The fruit is from the true vine that produces the new wine.

If you say, you love Mary then listen to Mary. She does not say, "Follow me, follow me", but "Follow him and do what he tells you to do." In 1Peter 1:23, Jesus is the imperishable seed: the living and abiding word of God from which we are born anew. When we listen to the Word and act on what he says, there is a transformation in us and we produce its fruit; God keeps the best wine until the last and all it takes is a simple yes, uttered in faith for us to change.

"Everyone who believes that Jesus is the Christ is begotten by God, and everyone who loves the father loves also the one begotten by him. In this way, we know we love the children of God when we love God and obey his commandments. Moreover, his commandments are not burdensome, for the one begotten of God conquers the world. And the victory that conquers the world is our faith." *(1John 5:1-5)*

We are baptised, prophet, priest, and king, and Mary is the model of who we already are in Jesus Christ when we have turned our life from what is the natural to the supernatural. Whatever we have filled our life with God can touch and turn it into something incredible just as he did with the water into wine at Cana.

If we accept this, we can walk away from whatever is our poverty and lack. Just as it was for the couple at the wedding feast who could only get so far on their own resources, we would have a banquet set before us in front of your foes and there will be no more scraps for God's people!

Faith is the ability to believe that the impossible is possible and then to go about doing it - faith is, doing it.

Chapter 16

Christian faith and the tripartite man

Beset on all sides with new age neo-gnostic spiritual concepts that often use Christian language to describe anything other than Christ and his teachings can cause us to become confused as to what makes man, man, and where our beliefs fit in. It now seems expedient to come down to earth and examine faith for our daily life to see how faith works.

In our drive for immortality, peace, security and successful living amidst an ever-growing atheist, neo-pagan, secular humanist and neo-gnostic world that has redesigned the concept of what makes man what he is as a human being and what constitutes our relationship with God and the cosmos he has created, it is essential to know our faith.

In 1Thessolonians 5:3 Saint Paul says that we are tripartite beings comprising body, soul and spirit. This is very much different from the dualist understanding before Vatican II. In the catechism following the Council of Trent, and particularly during the 19th and 20th centuries, it taught that we are body and soul. It described the soul as immortal and containing both spirit and mind. Therefore, properly understood, it does not contradict Saint Paul.

In order to grasp the operation of how faith comes, how it grows and how it acts, it is important that we approach it from a tripartite perspective and explain the relationship of the Trinity to man created in the image of God.

God, who is Spirit, made man in his own image and likeness. As we have noted previously in chapter two, the Hebrew understanding of the title *God* (*Elohim*) means, a single God in whom there is a plurality of persons and that the Hebrews did not have the fullness of revelation as we do through Jesus Christ but it is implicit in their understanding of plurality.

In prayer, many people can wonder to whom in the Trinity they are praying. The simple answer is that we are praying to the Father, through the Son, in the Holy Spirit. "The form now universal, 'Glory be to the Father, and to the Son, and to the Holy Spirit,' so clearly expresses the Trinitarian dogma that the Arians found it necessary to deny that it had been in use before the time of Flavian of Antioch. *(Philostorgius, "Hist. eccl.", III, xiii)*

It is true that up to the period of the Arian controversy another form, 'Glory to the Father, through the Son, in the Holy Spirit,' had been more common *(cf. I Clement, 58, 59; Justin "Apol.", I, 67)*. This latter form is indeed perfectly consistent with Trinitarian belief: it, however, expresses *not* the coequality of the Three Persons, *but their operation concerning man.* We live in the Spirit, and through Him, we are partakers in Christ *(Galatians 5:25; Romans 8:9)* and it is through Christ, as His members, that we are worthy to offer praise to God. *(Hebrews 13:15)*" - Dogma of the Trinity – New Advent Catholic Encyclopaedia

The action of the Trinity is present in the beginning of creation as we see in Genesis 1:26 and repeated John 1:1-3. Throughout the Old Testament the lives of the Prophets show the action of the Holy Spirit but he does not infill them or remain with them; he anoints for a purpose and then leaves. Although testified to in the Mazzaroth and the Old Testament that foreshadows the new, the Messiah revealed by God at the annunciation to Mary shows him to be Jesus sent from the Father and conceived of the Holy Spirit. *(John 13:3)* When the Holy Spirit descends upon Jesus at his baptism in the Jordan, the Father says of him, "This is my beloved son, with whom I am well pleased." *(Matthew 3:17, Luke 1:30-35)* The Father and the Holy Spirit give testimony that Jesus is the Son of God.

Throughout his ministry, Jesus glorifies the Father and makes him known. Later, Jesus reveals the Holy Spirit that is to fill and remain with his believers at Pentecost *(Acts 2:1-21)* and says in John 14: 16-26 that he will ask the Father to send another Advocate *(one like himself)* who will remain with them and reveal all truth reminding them of everything that Jesus has taught.

The Holy Spirit proceeds from both the Father and the Son and therefore, "a single God in whom there is a plurality of persons." In relationship to man, the Holy Spirit reveals the mind of God *(John 14:26)* and glorifies the Son, the Son reveals the Father and glorifies him and both glorify the Holy Spirit; all is to the glory of God the Father and all three are one and the same God coequal and yet distinct.

Perhaps Saint Patrick's three-leaf clover, the Shamrock, is a simple way to grasp that the Trinity is distinct persons in one God; there are three distinct parts but only a single plant. Man is also three distinct parts; body, soul and spirit; each part is distinct and defined according to its nature; the spirit operates in spiritual terms, the soul operates in intellectual and emotional terms and the body in physical terms.

Each is different, yet they are the same person and intrinsically connected in one nature, which is human; one separated from the other makes a man incomplete; the soul separated from the body results in death. The Trinity too is three distinct persons and yet one single God.

Another way we can get a simple grasp this triune oneness is by looking at one single man. If we only know a man's name, we could not say that we know him. If he told where he lived and what he did for an occupation, we would begin to know him better but could not say that we know him completely. If he said that he was a husband, a father, an uncle, a brother, a nephew, a son, a grandfather we would clearly understand that, although he was a different thing to different people, he is still only the one and same man.

If he then told us that he was a musician, an artist, an art director, a prayer group leader, and so on, he would still be the one and same man. In each role, he would function as the same person in the character of the relationship he was communicating at any given time.

By this plurality, we come to know him as the one person he is; the more things we know about a person, the more we know the person as one. Clearly, although the man is many things and many persons to different people depending on their relationship with him, he does not have multiple personalities - it is the one person relating in many different ways. It is the same with God; the Trinity reveals his oneness although three distinct persons. (254)

Throughout biblical history, God has been revealing his oneness expressed in the persons of the Trinity of which through Christ, we have the fullness of the revelation albeit remaining a mystery in the fullest sense that we as creatures will never be able to understand God fully.

Created in the divine image, man is also a trinity. He is firstly a created spirit being in the image of God who is Spirit. He has a soul that is the area of his intellect; will and emotions as God has a will and expresses emotions, and he lives in a body, as did the Word made flesh. The higher faculty of man is his spirit, the second is his soul that is akin to his spirit, and the lowest is his body. His spirit animates the soul and the body. This is the spirit that God breathed into him as dust and made him a living being. When man's spirit encounters the Word of God that is spirit and truth, it recognises the source of its existence and welcomes it; they become one.

The spirit of man driven to seek its origin is the natural journey of faith and the basis of religion. It is also the philosophical and scientific drive to understand his existence and to understand how his life and all life began.

Because we are by nature eternal, this same drive causes us to seek ways to prolong life and avoid the idea of death that is a foreign concept to our basic instincts. Although not fully conscious but hidden deep within, the instinct to avoid death is rooted in the reason we existed in the first place - even though separated from God, we still have this connection as a remnant left after the fall.

Even without knowledge of God, this remnant drives us to seek beyond ourselves. This drive causes us to seek God and we are not truly happy until we find him. This compulsion sets us on a journey as seekers of truth. Because man without reference to divine revelation is as it were, trying by his own effort, he can only climb so far before he reaches a limit.

In the case of Hinduism, and Buddhism as its offshoot, we find the concept of reincarnation. In simple terms, this is rooted in the idea of eternal life perceived from a terminal condition: a finite mind comprehending an infinite concept. In his own search, man cannot comprehend infinity within a finite mind. In order to do this he reasons that to become perfect is not possible in one lifetime, and one short lifetime defeats the remnant of his instinct for eternal life.

Every thought begins and ends. Every deed begins and ends. Everything related to our earthly existence begins and ends but the life around us continues without ending. Reincarnation is man understanding eternal life from a finite standpoint; in order to become infinite he must begin, end, begin, and end until, through successive lessons in successive lives, he reaches enlightenment, greater knowledge and perfections until finally ascending to the perfect eternal and infinite state.

A study of astronomy shows that the gods of man are the names of the planets that influenced all life and man's destiny on earth. These planet-gods could be either negative or positive. It was a strong belief that although everyone was born under the sun, the star sign or constellation in which the sun was located at the time of birth determined the influence on their lives.

In both Hinduism and Buddhism, we see this in a refined and developed way. Dalai Lamas of Buddhism discerned by the study of the horoscope *(Vedic Astrology)* are the ongoing reincarnation of the first Dalai Lama and presumably an incarnation of the Buddha. In Hinduism, we find that a guru reaching perfection ascends to a planetary domain. This idea is prevalent and especially so in the current New Age movement. When we seek God this way, we are inclined to perceive a god made in our own image and after our own likeness and, as these religions conclude, we are god.

The Christian understanding based on the tripartite nature of man in relationship to the Trinitarian nature of God goes beyond this earthbound concept of eternal life and the understanding of what makes man, man. This is due to the revelation that comes directly from God rather than man seeking to find and know God by his own efforts: God has reached man because man cannot reach God; the

102

Babylonians tried, corrupted the Mazzaroth and failed inciting the wrath of God. When we approach the idea of God, we are approaching that which in human terms is not possible by human knowledge alone.

The New Catholic Catechism teaches that faith is a gift from God and it refers to faith being a gift in order to believe that Jesus is Lord. It is right that we understand this as grace from God since by our own efforts we cannot comprehend the Divinity without God's help and guidance.

It is evident however, that everyone is born with openness to faith regardless of religious belief. It depends on what we put 'our' faith in that determines the outcome and the inevitable result. An example would be sitting down on a chair; we do not usually check to see if it will hold our weight and it does not become an issue unless it collapses. If it does collapse, we are shocked and surprised because without giving it another thought, we expected it to support us.

This system of belief in the adequacy of the chair comes to our understanding by the promises made by the manufacturer and made known to us through marketing. Because we believed what we heard regarding their promises, we simply sit down without further question. If only we could take God at his Word in the same way, his promises would overwhelm our lives and never let us down. After all, God is the architect of our lives and the manufacturer that offers a promise with an eternal guarantee; a guarantee signed in the eternal blood of his only Son, Jesus Christ and the way it works for us is found in the manufacturer's handbook; the Bible.

From the example of the chair, we can see that belief and faith is not the same thing. A person might believe that the chair would hold their weight but if they do not act on that belief, they will not sit down and find out that what they heard or believe is true. We might say we believe that God can heal but do nothing about it and remain sick. To illustrate this further let us suppose a man that is starving sits before a meal that could save his life. He looks at the meal and says I believe this meal will save me. I really believe this. I believe, I believe, I believe, but no action is taken to eat it, he will die. That is why we must act on what we say we believe because faith is belief in action, and faith without works is dead faith as Saint James tells us. *(James 2:14-26)*

The faith that the Catechism refers to is the supernatural ability that believes in order to have faith in Jesus Christ and to act in a manner that demonstrates that belief and so we need to *hear* about his promises no less than that of the chair. This is no different from believing in Marx, Buddha, Darwin, or anyone else when someone hears about them. The difference is that it takes grace, a gift, and an unearned favour to inspire us to put *our* faith in Jesus Christ and to accept who and what he says he is without doubt. This is an action of the Holy Spirit on our natural human faith: the same faith that enabled us to sit on a chair is the same faith that enables us to believe God.

The role of the Holy Spirit is to reveal the mind of God and to glorify Jesus, and this ordinarily happens through hearing about him either through preaching or reading the Bible, and perhaps, by reading this book.

Following the tripartite order of man as spirit, soul and body, we have to begin by understanding that our first experience of conscious reality is through our physical nature; even though you might be receiving spiritual insight as you are reading, you first perceive it through your eyes.

The words convey ideas and information understood by your mind. If the soul accepts them by reason and an act of the will, you will believe what you read and it will enter your spirit and become part of your faith. Because you believe, your faith will come through your spirit to your soul and it will become part of the speech and actions in your physical body.

We say *I see* when we understand something. When faith comes, we can see by faith rather than by physical sight the truth and realities presented to our soul by the Spirit of God, and so it is true to say that faith sees. When faith sees it believes. When faith believes it acts. When faith acts, it gets a result. If this faith is in God's Word then we see the result according to the Word. Faith and belief are interdependent in order to achieve this.

Chapter 17

The nature of light and the visible invisibility of faith

*T*he character of faith, like light, is invisible and yet it is tangible evidence of itself. The quality of light depends on the power of its source as the rays pass through or reflect the object that it strikes. The quality of the object determines the quality of light received by the eye: Rubber absorbs more light than chrome and therefore chrome is shiny while rubber is dull; chrome, as a mirror reflects more light and the disparity between light and shade is sharper in chrome than rubber.

When we look at the sky on a clear night, it is pitch black except for the moon and the stars. We say for example that the moon shines because it glimmers in the darkness. However, the moon does not shine of its own power and this is evident when we see a half moon; if it had the power to shine of its own accord, it would always be a full moon.

Unlike the moon, we do not see a half sun simply because the sun is the source and therefore complete within itself needing no other source of light to be visible in the darkness. In fact, the darkness cannot blot it out. What we see therefore is the reflection of the sun on the surface of the moon.

The distance between the sun and the moon that reflects it is black and yet the sun is still shining. At night, we can know that the sun is shining, not because we can see the sun or its light, but because we can see the moon and the stars that reflect it. During daylight, the same black sky is blue. This is only due to the sun's rays reflecting on the particles of the atmosphere. Therefore, the quality of daylight determined by the quality of the air gives us the different hues of blue or red at dawn or dusk and it is thus that we see the sky and those incredibly beautiful sunsets and sunrises.

Even during daylight hours, we do not see light, but rather that which reflects it; we can however see the source, which is the sun. At night, we can only see what reflects the sun and therefore we know by the evidence of the moon and stars that the sun is shining even though we cannot see it or the light rays emanating from it.

This is a metaphor for our relationship with God and what shows forth through our faith; it reflects our belief in God and the quality of faith that reflects it determines the quality of God that is manifest in our lives: God as the sun and we as the moon. Faith, like the rays of light from the sun is invisible, and in the same way, it is visible only by what it reflects. The quality of its reflection is the quality of the person reflecting it and the evidence of its presence. Faith like light is not visible unless it reflects our deeds.

A faith that has its source in man will reflect the words, deeds, and dispositions of man. In this case, reflected in the secular humanism and modernity of our days the results are clear for all to see; man is his own god and the morals and values reflect that disposition in all of society that acts according to its faith. Since its faith has no room for God, it has made itself a god. In doing so, its constitutions, oaths, and laws are removing all references to God in spite of the fact that the vast majority of people believe in God and western civilisation has become great in all sciences due to the Judeo-Christian ethic and moral laws.

A person that has faith in the teachings of the Buddha for example reflects it in their clothes, attitudes, dispositions, and actions. When we look at a Buddhist monk, we see by the saffron robes, the shaved head and bodily postures that he reflects the Buddha in whom he believes and has faith. When he speaks, he reflects the teachings of the Buddha. If he is well conformed to those teachings then he will reflect more of the source of those teachings in his total life expression. A person who espouses atheism will reflect atheism in the same way.

Whatever a person puts their faith in will determine what comes out. In other words, faith is visible only by the outward expressions that reflect it. The fruit the tree bears tells us what it is. The seed might look like any other, the tree might look like any other, but when the fruit appears, we know what tree it really is, and the quality of the fruit it produces will reflect the quality of the tree and the soil in which it is rooted. It is not surprising then that Jesus can refer to faith as a seed and he as the light without contradiction.

Planted in the soil of a good heart the seed of faith in God's Word reflects more of its source as it bears fruit and we become the light of the world, a light that more clearly reflects its source that is Jesus and the Word of God, the true light in whom we are firmly rooted. A seed cannot grow without the light of the sun and neither can we without the light of faith. The origin of faith is God and therefore all faith, like the seed, seeks the light. Another way to put this is, like attracts its likeness.

We walk by faith, not by sight and therefore the source of our faith is God who is invisible and yet gives light to all things including life itself. That is how the visible universe displays the invisible attributes of an unseen God and we as his children reflect the hidden attributes of his

108

glory. "No one has seen God. The only Son, God, who is at the Father's side, has revealed him." *(John 1:18)* Jesus fully reflected God and so he could say that to see him was to see the Father. He is the perfect reflection of the invisible God visible in human form. *(Colossians 1:15)* "He reflects the brightness of God's glory and is the exact likeness of God's own being, *sustaining the universe with his powerful word.* After achieving forgiveness for the sins of all human beings, he sat down in heaven at the right side of God, the Supreme Power." *(Hebrews 1:3)*

When we, by faith in his Word, become conformed to what he says, we too reflect that light for all to see and can therefore accomplish the things that he accomplished in his ministry. We are like light for the whole world. A city on a hill cannot hide and we reflect the light of Christ. *(Matthew 5:14)* These accomplishments are the signs that point to the source, Jesus himself. We are thus walking in the light of faith, and the way in which people perceive us is the way they perceive the invisible God in whom we believe.

It is through our words and actions that those without faith can grasp something of what they cannot see and so Saint Paul calls us ambassadors. An ambassador represents the country to which he belongs and therefore to know him is to know that country. The ambassador reflects the values and culture of the country he represents. Because the people to whom he presents himself cannot see the country from which he comes, the ambassador is the tangible evidence of what they cannot see; if he misrepresents his government, others receive a false impression. If they believe this to be true, then they will treat that government accordingly.

Our conformity to the Word of God determines the purity of God that others perceive through our words and actions. If our words fall short, so does their perception of the God we proclaim. If our deeds fall short, so does their perception of the truth we attempt to demonstrate.

A way to explain this is to imagine the sun. It is so bright that we cannot look upon it and even though the function of our eyes is to receive light, they will go blind if we do not turn away; they are not capable of receiving that much intensity directly. If we wish to look upon the sun, we need to use filters to protect our eyes. In the same way, we cannot look upon God, but we can see what reflects him and what he reveals to us either directly by revelation or through creation. In order for God to show himself to us he sent Jesus because we cannot look directly upon the Father without destruction; the sin we carry makes us incapable.

In the beginning, God accomplished this by the blood covenant he made with Adam in Genesis 3:21 when he made leather garments for Adam and Eve. Their own attempt using fig leaves after the fall could not cause them to approach God because it could not hide the sin: the sin that is the darkness in them and in which they now dwelt. Many people try to cover or excuse their misdeeds by their own efforts. This is like clothing themselves with a fig leaf; it might do the job in the short term, but when fall *(autumn)* comes, so falls the leaf to their great embarrassment.

We cannot hide from God anymore than the moon can hide from the sun unless something comes between them. The leather garment meant that when God came to them as pure light as was his custom with Adam, it would not destroy them due to the darkness in them. God therefore covered their sin so he did not have to look upon it. He could then communicate because the light, filtered out so to speak, enabled them to approach the light and the light to approach them: The blood bridged the gap and the leather garment was the veil that filtered out the light.

This approach became the way in which God would appear to man throughout the Old Testament. The use of blood covenants enabled God to approach man because the sacrifices covered the sin. However, whilst this made a bridge, it did not repair the gap or take away the cause. To do this God sent Jesus in the likeness of sinful flesh as expiation for sin in order to repair the breach. Because God was now in human form, it was possible for us to look upon him without destruction, as would our eyes looking at the sun. God could also communicate directly with man without the need for an intermediary. Jesus in human form, the flesh, was the filter so to speak.

On Mount Tabor Jesus revealed the source of the true light at his Transfiguration. When Jesus died on Calvary, he removed the veil; the leather garment, the gap, and repaired the breach. From that moment, man was able to approach God directly in the spirit without destruction. However, until the final resurrection we cannot approach God without an intermediary due to our sin.

God cannot look upon sin; he turns his face away from us when we approach him. Jesus as the mediator and advocate stands between God and us. God then looks upon the scars and blood of Jesus. Jesus tells the Father to look at the scars upon his body and tells the Father that he has paid the price. The Holy Spirit, the other Advocate (Council for the defence) testifies to this because the Spirit and the Word agree and God accepting their testimony accepts us and we can then approach him as though we had not sinned.

Justified through faith in the passion and cross of Jesus Christ who is the expiation of our sin is what Saint Paul calls righteousness and justification; Jesus has exchanged our righteousness that is as filthy rags for his own robe of righteousness, and this why Saint Paul can say that we are the righteousness of God in Christ Jesus. "But we are all as an unclean thing, and all our righteousness is as filthy rags; and we all do fade as a leaf; and our iniquities, like the wind, have taken us away." *(Isaiah 64:6)*

Righteousness is an old English word that means to be in right standing with the king. Because Jesus Christ has removed our sin, we have right standing with God and so with faith in him will now look upon the face of God and live.

In this life, we still see as through a glass darkly as Saint Paul puts it, but then we will see him as he really is. *(1Corinthians 13:12)* At the beatific vision, God will reveal his glory and we will see him in his true form. At the same time, we will be resplendent in our glory, a glory that comes from Jesus Christ who has purified us through his Word. Presently, only the light of faith knows this. The veil removed for those that accept Jesus Christ, allows us look upon God and approach the throne of Grace to obtain mercy and timely help in our daily life. *(Hebrews 4:14-16)*

Catholic apologist Raymond de Souza, founder of Saint Gabriel Communications in Perth Western Australia, points out that as much as the Transfiguration of Jesus on Mount Tabor was a miracle when Jesus shone in resplendent glory, the real miracle was that Jesus did not shine all the time. This is because to shine in glory is Jesus' true expression of himself and natural state, for he is God and he is Light. Raymond also points out that the real miracle of the Eucharist is that it too does not shine. Since Christ is present fully, its natural state is to shine in glory.

When we adore Christ present in the Eucharist, it is a sublime act of faith because we cannot see that shining light of glory and yet we believe that Christ the light is present to us. An even greater act of faith is the reception of the Eucharist in Holy Communion. It is here that heaven and earth are united, man and God are one together in glory and that presents another miracle in that, for that short moment of time, man does not shine and yet the glory of the Lord is present in the tabernacle of his heart. The time will come when we will see God as he is and look upon his face, but until then, we see by faith and not by sight. *(Luke 9:28-36)*

When we become one with Jesus as he had prayed in John 17: 20, we, like the moon in direct line with the sun, will be seen in our fullness as we reflect the light of Christ. When we turn away, even in the smallest increments, we like the moon, will wax and wane into complete darkness until we turn once more to face the sun because we have no light of our own to sustain us.

We can only know ourselves fully in our reality in the light of the reality of God. Without this, nothing else makes sense, especially the reason that we exist as the only speck of sub atomic dust in the universe that can ponder this idea in the first place.

Chapter 18

Faith, spiritual warfare and a visibly invisible shield

*I*n physics, we know there is no such thing as darkness, only an absence of light. For example, when we enter a dark room and switch on the light, the darkness vanishes. Not even the sum total of the darkest night can overcome and extinguish even the weakest light. It is the same with faith; a mustard seed is enough to dispel the darkness or move a mountain.

The Word of God like a seed as Jesus described, is the switch that connects the power to our soul and dispels the darkness of sin. To be free of sin our faith needs to be in his Word so that we walk in the light of faith and not the darkness of our sin and unbelief. The quality of light that we see in the natural world is in direct proportion to the quality of the object that reflects it or through which it passes.

It is the same with us. The Word of God cleanses us in the bath of rebirth and the longer we spend in the Word the more pure is the light that we reflect. As in the natural order, so too in the supernatural, for it is accepted that grace builds on nature: first the natural and then the supernatural. *(1Corinthians 15:45-49)*

The degree of light that we see is also in the direct proportion to that through which it passes before reaching our eyes. If the sun's rays pass through a clean window, we see a purer light but if the same rays pass through a frosted or dirty window, we see much less of the light's quality. It is in such a way that sin frosts the windows of our soul and therefore it filters out the light of God. If a window became dirty enough it would block out all the light, and the room, by its absence, would be in complete darkness.

This is what happens when we allow even the smallest sin to prevail. At first, it might not look much and maybe, like a speck of dust on the window, it seems to make no difference. However, if we leave it, we will adjust to it, and because we can still see the light through the windowpane, we will do nothing. Eventually, that little speck of sin will attract other specks and before we know it, we will be walking in darkness stumbling over the furniture to find the light switch. The window-cleaner for our soul is our faith in the Word of God and the more we rub it in the cleaner it becomes.

Sin is the agent of death and death is the absence of life. We are created immortal beings destined to live forever. The notion of death as the final extinction of our life is foreign to our nature otherwise there would no hell or eternal damnation; if we did not exist after death, there would be no one to punish. The concept of life after death is a basic tenet of all religions. This would seem due to the divine image inherent within us.

Although far removed from its origin, the motivational force deep within seeks to live longer and ponders the mystery of life because death is contrary to our basic instinct for survival. It would be true then to say that death is merely an absence of life, a life separated from God its source and destiny but not extinguished.

Some theologians take this a step further and say, that evil is only an absence of good. If this is relating to Lucifer's rebellion, then we could say that evil existed because of an absence of good in Lucifer except that God created all things good including Lucifer. In fact, the word Lucifer means, "Light Bearer" and so there was no darkness in him at his creation because there is no darkness in God.

As a creature, Lucifer, as with all the angels, had to choose salvation. An angelic will is direct, instant, and irrevocable. When Lucifer chose against God, he left the light, lost the name Lucifer, and became Devil or Satan; prince of darkness. *(Isaiah 14:12)* In this case, it would be true to say that the evil now present in Lucifer was an absence of good. However, it is not true to say that evil as a force is an absence of good because that would mean that the devil does not exist, whereas The Roman Rite of Exorcism clearly says, "Evil is not something, but someone."

In addition, it would say that Satan is an equal and opposite of God because evil is the opposite of good, and that is simply not so due to the fact that God created Lucifer; therefore as the agent of evil, Lucifer cannot be equal to God. The Bible teaches us to conquer evil with good and so it is clear according to God that good is superior to any form of evil.

This *someone* is the source and origin of evil and he can only attack the human mind by means of temptations to freely accept what he offers be it either power or the attractions of sin. Temptations in themselves are not sins; just because a person is grievously tempted does not mean that they have sinned. However, the devil's attacks begin to convince the soul that because it feels so wretched it has already sinned, and thus convinced, the person accepts the deception and chooses to act. It is only then that sin exists for that person.

The truth is that the devil cannot make us sin; we do that by choosing to act on the temptation, and all too often, without his help at all. The devil did not make Adam and Eve sin because he could not make them do anything

116

against their free will. His tactic was distortion of truth, deception, and temptation focussing their attention on the tree of the knowledge of good and evil, and he still works the same way today.

A satanic lie is not always a complete untruth; often it has a percentage of truth in it; for example, it might be 2% truth and 98% lie. According to Saint Thomas Aquinas, "man's natural tendency is towards the good" and so we accept the small percentage of truth and swallow lie. Most often, a satanic lie is a gross exaggeration or gross distortion of a fact that sounds correct due to the kernel of truth left in it as it was in Eden regarding the two trees and as we see in the occult zodiacal corruption of the Mazzaroth.

Satanism in general is growing with alarming popularity, especially amongst the young and we are seeing more manifestations that are demonic. In the USA we find the, *Church of Satan* founded on April 30, 1966 by Anton Szandor LaVey. This quote with their capital letters from the introduction on their web site reads, "We are the first above-ground organization in history openly dedicated to the acceptance of Man's true nature—that of a carnal beast, living in a cosmos which is permeated and motivated by the Dark Force which we call Satan.

Over the course of time, Man has called this Force by many names, and those have reviled it whose very nature causes them to be separate from this fountainhead of existence. They live in obsessive envy of we who exist by flowing naturally with the dread Prince of Darkness. It is for this reason that individuals who resonate with Satan have always been an alien elite, often outsiders in cultures whose masses pursue solace in an external deity. We Satanists are our own Gods, and we are the explorers of the Left-Hand Path. We do not bow down before the myths and fictions of the desiccated spiritual followers of the Right-Hand Path."

Whilst it would be wrong to point only to this organisation regarding satanic activity, it is interesting to note that it is first legitimate organisation in the USA with full tax exemption rights. Only mentioned here due to its manifesto it sums up the full sin nature of man exalting himself and the cosmos to the heights of a deity. No, this is not from a bygone age of myths and fairy tales, it is a reality in our days; there are many such organisations and groups that worship Satan as well as practice his dark arts.

While on mission in England some years ago, a man said that, "Part of the problem is that Satan is building his army while the Christians are entertaining themselves." How true this is. It seems to be the reverse of what happened in the first four centuries. At that time, the Christians were building a spiritual army while the Romans were entertaining themselves and we all know the outcome of that situation.

In our days, we are witnessing a spiritual phenomenon that is unique in history, as there does not seem to have been a revival of spiritual evil in such a socially acceptable manner as we are seeing today. Sadly, over time, many theological speculations have discarded the notion of Satan as a real and living being and so it would seem that when the Church lets its shield down, the devil runs amok and takes the high ground.

In spite of this, it does not seem to be a coincidence that at the rise of occult beliefs and practices along with astrology, witchcraft, magic, alchemy and satanism on a global scale, that there is also a rise in the activity of the Holy Spirit within the Church. This demonstrates that there are two worldviews in conflict. Whilst the world is turning increasingly to the worship of nature and the self, there has also been a rise of grace by the Holy Spirit that in the Catholic Church began in the same year as the opening of

Vatican II and has been instrumental in renewing the faith of millions.

Beginning with a small group of students and staff in February 1967 at Duquesne University, USA, the Catholic Charismatic Renewal has grown in excess of a hundred million adherents around the world as at the time of writing. It has spread like fire across the world and thus accepted as the fastest growing movement in the Church today and serves to demonstrate that where sin abounds, grace abounds even more.

The Catholic Charismatic Renewal does not claim a founder or visionary with direct access to God and therefore it is not a cult and presents the Charismatic gifts *(supernatural endowments of the Holy Spirit)* as normal and available to everyone. It expresses that healing and miracles are ordinary Christianity because it is a renewal of what we already are in Christ. In addition, it does not claim these supernatural endowments as a sign of holiness as can happen with some current visionaries and seers.

Although there have been abuses of the gifts of the Spirit just as there was in Corinth during Saint Paul's time largely through ignorance, this does not occur in general. Its members do not claim to be extraordinary or seers even though they can deliver God's message to people or the Church through the prophetic gifts of the Spirit and experience amazing healings.

A genuine move of the Holy Spirit will establish that the miraculous is in fact normal Christianity available to every baptised Christian, and no personal claim or impressions of being specially chosen by God will occur.

This charismatic movement of the Holy Spirit is not the only authentic renewal within the Church of course, but it is unique and it should give us hope because it functions predominantly at the grass roots level of the laity. Blessed

119

and accepted by the Popes, it points to the spiritual weapons needed in this present darkness, in particular the Corinthian gifts, a resurgence of the five-fold ministries of prophet, apostle, preacher, teacher, evangelist and pastor. In addition, it empowers people for a love of the Church, the Bible and a life committed to Jesus Christ in a dynamic way while striving for a life of holiness.

The laity, particularly exposed to New Age influences in their daily lives, face great challenges to their faith, yet at the same time they are at the forefront of spiritual warfare, and as a result, they are a formidable army for Jesus Christ. No wonder the devil is doing all he can to undermine doctrine and faith to prevent this; he has established on earth what I call *A Paradise of Hell* and a whole system of counterfeit gifts for his counterfeit kingdom along with counterfeit gods. Those so caught up and deluded by this religious spirit where for them no sin exists, think they are in paradise but in reality, they are already in hell on earth.

Since the turn of the nineteenth century, Christian revivals have sprouted, some genuine and others somewhat suspect and short lived. Never the less this parallels the rise in occult activity and not the least of which is through Madam Blavatsky's Theosophical Society. Thankfully, the Church has now begun to expose this for what it is and says, "The essential matrix of New Age thinking is to be found in the esoteric-theosophical tradition which was fairly widely accepted in European intellectual circles in the 18th and 19th centuries. It was particularly strong in freemasonry, spiritualism, occultism and theosophy, which shared a kind of esoteric culture.

In this world-view, the visible and invisible universes link by a series of correspondences, analogies and influences between microcosm and macrocosm, between metals and planets, between planets and the various parts of the human body, between the visible cosmos and the invisible realms of reality. Nature is a living being shot through with networks of sympathy and antipathy, animated by a light and a secret fire, which human beings seek to control. People can contact the upper or lower worlds by means of their imagination *(an organ of the soul or spirit)* or by using mediators *(angels, spirits, devils)* or rituals.

People can be initiated into the mysteries of the cosmos, god and the self by means of a spiritual itinerary of transformation. The eventual goal is gnosis, the highest form of knowledge, the equivalent of salvation. It involves a search for the oldest and highest tradition in philosophy *(inappropriately called philosophia perennis)* and religion *(primordial theology)*, a secret *(esoteric)* doctrine, which is the key to all the "exoteric" traditions, and accessible to everyone. Esoteric teachings are handed down from master to disciple in a gradual program of initiation."

It continues by saying, "Some see 19th century esotericism as completely secularised. Alchemy, magic, astrology and other elements of traditional esotericism are thoroughly integrated with aspects of modern culture, including the search for causal laws, evolutionism, psychology and the study of religions. It reached its clearest form in the ideas of Helena Blavatsky, a Russian medium who founded the Theosophical Society with Henry Olcott in New York in 1875.

The Society aimed to fuse elements of Eastern and Western traditions *(religions)* in an evolutionary type of spiritualism. It had three main aims: *1:* to form a nucleus of the Universal Brotherhood of Humanity, without distinction of race, creed, caste or colour. *2:* to encourage the study of comparative religion, philosophy and science. *3:* to investigate unexplained laws of nature and the powers latent in man.

The significance of these objectives should be clear. The first objective implicitly rejects the 'irrational bigotry' and 'sectarianism' of traditional Christianity as perceived by spiritualists and theosophists. It is not immediately obvious from the objectives themselves that, for theosophists, 'science' meant the occult sciences and philosophy the occulta philosophia, that the laws of nature were of an occult or psychic nature, and that comparative religion was expected to unveil a 'primordial tradition' ultimately modelled on a Hermeticist philosophia perennis.

A prominent component of Mrs. Blavatsky's writings was the emancipation of women, which involved an attack on the "male" God of Judaism, of Christianity and of Islam. She urged people to return to the mother-goddess of Hinduism and to the practice of feminine virtues. This continued under the guidance of Annie Besant, who was in the vanguard of the feminist movement. Wicca and 'women's spirituality' carry on this struggle against 'patriarchal' Christianity today." *(The essential matrix of New Age thinking - A Christian reflection on the "New Age" Pontifical Council for Culture Pontifical Council for Interreligious Dialogue)*

Due to the increasing problem with the demonic, magic and occult activity, the Church has also begun to address the problem in a decisive way. In February 2005 Catholic on-line news agency Zenit.org reported a new course on "Satanism, Exorcism and the Prayer of Liberation" that is being offered for clergy formation on guiding souls in contact with the occult or magic. Giuseppe Ferrari, secretary of the Group of Research and Information on the Sects *(GRIS)* of Italy, commented on the objects of the course, which began at the Regina Apostolorum Pontifical Athenaeum.

Giuseppe Ferrari told Zenit that the first aspect to consider is that of vocation. A priest who does not have a profound and genuine vocation will never be able to be an authentic and authoritative spiritual guide for the community entrusted to him. A second aspect is that of formation. He said that this task, by which priests learn to distinguish and reject philosophical, doctrinal, theological and historical errors and biblical misinterpretation, constitutes a duty that we cannot defer, as the sects are spreading in the Catholic realm.

He said this is taking advantage not only of people's needs and of aspirations, but also falsifying history, manipulating and erroneously interpreting sacred Scripture, introducing unacceptable theological theses, debatable doctrines, and rash philosophical theses.

The new apologetics must not cause clashes but be open to profound, lucid and flexible dialogue. It must be able to relate to the different disciplines: theological, philosophical, historical, scientific, economic, artistic, etc., and project the truth to illuminate the different human problems and offer the man of today solid reasons for Christian hope.

To offer future priests a balanced and profound theological, moral and spiritual formation will serve to avoid, or at least reduce considerably, the risk of having presbyters who are seduced by risky theological speculations, or liturgical and pastoral experimentations with undeniably syncretistic connotations.

He said that the Church is in ever-greater need of holy priests, not of priests who preach ambiguous theological theses and strange liturgical and pastoral practices. This was because only holy priests are able to renew the Church, giving her new sap and new vigour, and the capacity to indicate the necessary impulses to initiate the correct responses to the different challenges of contemporary society.

Lastly, in this situation, which the spread of magic and superstitious religiosity has contributed to generate, is the ever more urgent need for priests to impart blessings to cancel the negative effects of alleged curses or to exercise the ministry of exorcism on those allegedly possessed by the devil. The requests are increasingly numerous and create notable problems for the clergy and dioceses, as in these areas priestly formation has been very lacking or nonexistent lately. It is also opportune to fill this gap.

He says one of the best ways to proceed, is not to appoint an exorcist who would then be overwhelmed by requests to which he could not respond. Or to appoint a diocesan commission made up of experts in some fields *(for example, in addition to the theological-pastoral, the medical and psychological)* but above all to form in this specific area a great number of priests, and said that this is the main objective of the course. *(Zenit.org article reference ZE05021829 February 18 2005)*

This is very encouraging indeed but in our daily lives, there is much to contend with as we try to live our Christian lives in the midst of such opposition. We would do well to remember that our battle is not against flesh and blood but with the principalities, with the powers, with the world rulers of this present darkness, with evil spirits in the heavens above.

In his letter to the Ephesians Saint Paul draws up our battle plan and he lists out battle armour and weapons. Significantly, he refers to faith as a shield that will extinguish the fiery arrows of the evil one. Conversely, a shield lying on the ground will do no good, we must take it up, that is, take up our faith for without it we are defenceless in the spiritual warfare in which we can often to our dismay, find ourselves.

The shield we take up is no ordinary shield; it is the invisibly visible shield of faith; to us it is invisible and we can see through it when we hold it up, but it is visible to Satan, for the shield is God himself. We cannot see God, but Satan can, as Saint Paul says, "You are hidden in Christ." Because Satan, as previously stated, is a fallen angel and formally called Lucifer, meaning, "Light Bearer" he can see God directly. God is light and so the shield is fully revealed and present to Satan's sight.

As for us, the shield is invisible and so we must accept that God is present to us by faith, and when we hold up our faith, God sees it and acts on our behalf as he did for the Israelites when they held up faith.

In the blood covenant with Abraham, the scar is in the penis. In Hebrew, the word covenant means to 'cut where blood flows.' All the nations around the Israelites practiced blood covenants and the sign and seal was the scar usually cut into the palm of the hand. When under attack, a person travelling alone would hold up the covenant scar to signify to his attackers that he was in covenant with another. Because his enemy did not know how powerful that covenant partner was, they would back off and let him travel in peace; the scar held up was the only protection needed.

In the case of the Israelites, it was not possible to hold up the scar when attacked. Because God is a hidden God, the scar of the covenant was in a hidden place. The mark of their covenant with Yahweh, demonstrated by holding up their faith caused God to act. God, seeing their faith, would act on their behalf. God is the invisibly visible shield and it is not by coincidence that Saint Paul uses the example of armour to refer to God's protection.

Abraham was the man of faith that God accounted as righteous. When God approached Abram at the

125

beginning of the blood covenant ritual, he knew that Abram understood covenant and that it involved an exchange. In Genesis 15:1, God says, "Fear not Abram! I am your shield." Because God does not have real armour to give, he gives himself. God's armour is himself, Abram accepts it by faith, and God continues to cut the covenant with him.

In Ephesians 6:10-17, God not only offers us himself as a shield, but as a complete suit of armour. This is what I call the covenant armour of God given to us through Jesus Christ; he exchanges our feeble, dull and rusty armour for his own so that unlike Don Quixote we are alert to the nature of the conflict and win over our enemy rather than battling inanimate windmills.

We put on the breastplate of righteousness, the helmet of the hope of our salvation, the belt of truth and the shoes of the gospel but we take up the shield of faith and the sword of the Spirit that is the Word of God. In other words, the shield is faith and the sword of the Spirit is the Word of God *(Rhema)* when we speak it and thus being "doers of the Word," we are more able to achieve our desired result. *(Ephesians 6:10-17)*

Defeated on Calvary, Satan will not fight Jesus again and when we hold our faith up, he backs off. Satan also backs off when we give our lives to Christ – we are too hot, enthusiastic and focussed on Jesus and so he keeps his distance waiting for us to cool down, and when we become lukewarm – he strikes.

Faith in the Word of God protects us from the tactics of the evil one and so it is imperative that we have a clear knowledge and understanding of exactly what God has said and what he means by it. Naturally, we must read and understand the Bible in order to respond as God desires and instructs for an effective outcome. Certainly by this means, we will not be easily influenced or confused when the enemy tries to ensnare us with his distorted truths as we will, as the Apostle says, rightly divide falsehood and truth rather than relying entirely on our own means.

"For although we are in the flesh, we do not battle according the flesh, for the weapons of our battle are not of flesh but are enormously powerful, capable of destroying fortresses. We destroy arguments and every pretension raising itself against the knowledge of God, and take every thought into captivity in obedience to Christ..." *(2Corinthians 10:3-5)* In the Lord's Prayer Jesus says, "Deliver us of from the evil one."

Chapter 19

Creation responds to the
Word of God spoken in faith

aint Paul says the whole of creation is in the pangs of
childbirth awaiting the revelation of the sons of God.
(Romans 8:19) Faith destroys all distance between God
and man and therefore our faith in Jesus Christ repairs the
damage caused by sin. Restored into fellowship with our
Creator we again reflect the divine image and creation
responds to us obediently once more. *(John 5:14)*

Due to this restoration, we can now perform the
works of Christ in the realm of the miraculous; God gives us
power *(Greek, dumanis; miraculous power, ability, abundance, might, strength,
mighty works)* from on high by the agency of the Holy Spirit to
do the works of Christ and yet, even the greater. *(Acts 1:8; John
14:12)*

John 14:10-12 says, "Do you not believe that I am in
the Father and the Father is in me? The words *(the Rhema)* that
I speak to you I do not speak on my own. The Father who
dwells in me is doing the works. Believe me that I am in the
Father and the Father is in me, or else, believe because of the
works *(Rhema)* themselves. Amen, amen, I say to you,
whoever believes in me shall do the works that I do, and
will do greater ones than these, because I am going to the
Father."

Jesus is saying that the Logos and the Rhema are the
same; The Logos made flesh in Jesus becomes Rhema when

Jesus speaks and acts on what the Logos reveals to him in his humanity.

When we accept the Word of God, it accomplishes in us what God intended. Those who do such are what John's Gospel calls, 'his own', for they recognise his voice and obey it. This is why Jesus is the alpha and the omega; the beginning and the end; first and the last; all things are summed up in him and our separation caused through Adam's sin is restored through our faith in Jesus. He is the new Adam and he makes all things new, and that especially means you.

This is paramount and significant for us; it animates our faith in a dynamic way because when we are conformed to Christ by the Word of God, creation recognises the Word that holds it in being; it responds accordingly as it did for Jesus and as it did at the beginning when God first spoke it into existence.

Our faith in the Word of God activates the Word as we speak it. We say to a disease, "In the name of Jesus leave this body." Alternatively, we might pray that a broken bone returns to health. Both the disease and the bone are of the same sub-atomic structure in differing forms and both are obedient to the Word that created them when spoken by us in faith.

We see this regarding Simon's mother-in-law in Luke 4: 38-39, "After he left the synagogue, he entered the house of Simon. Simon's mother-in-law was afflicted with a severe fever, and they interceded with him about her. He stood over her, rebuked the fever, and it left her." We note that Jesus spoke directly to the fever.

With faith in the name of Jesus and conformed to his Word by faith, we can do the same and expect the same result. Of course, we know that speaking such is not an ignorant act or some sort of superstitious magical spell; it is a result of a close relationship with God in Christ. It is also faith in His Name as power of attorney and a developed knowledge of his will through the Word of God empowered by the Holy Spirit. Even though, until we are perfect in our faith we do not always see a direct result, we have the guarantee that the least we can expect is a blessing from God, and God's blessing is the substance of the result we desire.

Often we are disappointed because when we pray this way, we do not see an instantaneous healing. If this is your experience, it does not invalidate the truth of God's Word nor does it necessarily invalidate your faith. Jesus said in Mark 16: 18, "...They will lay hands on the sick, and they will recover." It is important to grasp the promise of recovery that implies a period of time rather than an instantaneous result every time we pray. This requires that we persist in faith believing without seeing and never failing in the hope that we look for and thanking God always for his promise until it comes.

A modern day example is that of Olga, mentioned in the Slovenian translation of 12 Steps to Divine Healing, who was bleeding to death from leukaemia in a hospital in Penang, Malaysia, and only had hours to live.

During an altar call at a healing rally at the Immaculate Conception Catholic Church, two young women came forward begging God to heal their older sister who was dying in a local hospital. The two sisters had flown from India a few days previously after hearing that Olga was in the last stages of leukaemia and was on the verge of dying. Not able to go with them to the hospital due to commitments they were comforted and I led them in a prayer of agreement *(Matthew 18:19)* that even though we were not present to Olga, Jesus was, and he could touch her with healing in the hospital where she lay.

The following night the sisters returned in great distress. As soon as I was available after praying with some hundred people or so, they again pleaded with me to go to the hospital. Olga's condition had grown worse overnight and she was now bleeding to death. Due to speaking commitments that evening, and all the next day at a conference, it was not possible to go with them and so I gave them a phone number to call should another more serious emergency arise.

The next day after I had preached five one-hour sessions, the phone call came with a heartfelt plea to go to the hospital. Immediately cancelling a meeting with community elders, I went to pray for Olga taking with me fellow evangelist, Steve Peake.

At the hospital, the two sisters and Olga's daughter were waiting anxiously in the main entrance. They ran to me crying profusely saying, "She's dying and now her kidneys have stopped working and she cannot stop bleeding. She is in emergency now. Please help us!" Seeing their desperation, I said, "Take me to her." and they led the way to wait for Olga's return.

Once there, we prayed and waited for Olga to be brought back from emergency. We comforted Olga's daughter and the two sisters until Olga arrived suddenly with nurses and orderlies pushing her bed. We entered the elevator with her and those two floors to the ward was the longest and hardest journey ever; as her sisters cried and shook with fear, Olga lay motionless and exceedingly ill.

After settling Olga into her bed, the nurses left the room. Steve and I encouraged her daughter and sisters to have faith and invited everyone to join in agreement that Olga would recover when I prayed for her.

While Steve prayed with and encouraged her daughter and sisters, I went to Olga. She was barely

131

conscious as I lent close to her ear and explained why I was there. "Olga, do you want me to pray for you?" I asked. She uttered a weak, 'yes'. "Olga, do you believe that Jesus is bigger than this disease and that he can remove it from your body?" Another weak 'yes' came from Olga's lips, "So do I. Olga, all I want you to do now is, as best as you can understand how, receive what God gives to you as I pray, and trust him, because he loves you, and he will begin to work a blessing into your body."

As Olga gave a slight nod, I began to pray boldly for health and life to enter Olga's body in the Name of Jesus addressing the cancerous cells in her blood. At the same time, everyone began to pray in tongues.

Steve had exhorted the others to expect something good to happen - and happen, it did! While I was praying, the door opened and her doctor came in and left. Undisturbed by this, I kept praying, when suddenly the whole atmosphere changed. In an instant the room filled with light, everyone cheered up and Olga began to praise Jesus, "Thank you Jesus, thank you Jesus! Praise you Jesus!" She exclaimed as the prayer in tongues turned to joyful thanks.

Olga was now conscious and the colour of death in her flesh vanished as the colour of health returned to her face. At this point, I moved away as the sisters rushed to hug Olga who, although tired, was smiling as she praised God for what he had done for her.

Two weeks later, I received an email that said, "Olga is recovering... She is so much better than the first time you saw her. She is so full of love and she is praising the Lord so very boldly and loudly. She says she's healed 110% and her promise to the Lord is that she'll start a ministry by opening her home to anyone, the young and the old, just to learn to love and praise God."

Whether or not Olga's recovery was a coincidence or God's intervention may not seem certain. What is certain however is that she was on the verge of death, and there was a dramatic change during prayer. Sent home two days later, Olga had a clean bill of health. This could only happen by faith in the promises of Christ. This faith justifies us and makes us righteous before God who is, by virtue of our faith in him, pleased.

The ability to please God comes by faith in what Jesus has said; when we act on the Word of God, the Logos becomes Rhema in us. Thus restored to God's favour we see the results in answered prayers and successful endeavours as we reflect the divine image. Creation recognises this and responds with obedience as to its Creator. *(James 3:14-22)*

James 5:13-18 speaks eloquently of praying for the sick saying that the *prayer of faith* in the name of the Lord will save the sick person. In doing so the Lord will raise them up, and if they have committed sins, God will forgive them. He goes on to say, "The fervent prayer of a righteous man is very powerful."

Righteousness is an old English word that simply means to be in right standing with the king. Our faith gives us right standing with the King of kings and his royal sceptre gives us the King's ear that listens to our plea. Regarding creation, James 5: 17-18 says, "Elijah was a human being like us; yet he prayed earnestly that it might not rain, and for three years and six months it did not rain upon the land. Then he prayed again, and the sky gave rain and the earth produced its fruit."

Take courage therefore, the great prophet Elijah who was taken up to heaven in fiery chariot was a human being like you, so take a lesson from Elijah and pray earnestly, for all of creation is longing to hear from you too.

133

Even though we must die and return to dust, never the less, by virtue of our immortal soul and the Holy Spirit in us, who is the Lord and giver of life we do not see death, but pass from life into eternal life. "If the Spirit of the one who raised Jesus from the dead dwells in you, the one who raised Jesus from the dead will give life to your mortal bodies also, through the Spirit that dwells in you." *(Romans 8:11)*

The Word of God by the Holy Spirit that is in us raises even our mortal bodies from death and seats us with Christ in heavenly places, for where he is, there are we also. We are one with him and the prayer of Jesus in John 17:20-21 reaches its conclusion. Created anew, our physical body reflects the image and likeness of the new Adam. Recreated as a new creature in Christ we are ready for the new heaven and a new earth even in this life. Thus, we reign with him forever having inherited his Kingdom by faith as joint heirs with Jesus Christ.

This however is not the case for "the unfaithful, the cowards, the depraved, murderers, the unchaste, sorcerers, idol-worshippers, and the deceivers of every sort; their lot is in the burning pool of fire and sulphur, which is the second death." *(Revelations 21:1-8; Revelation 22: 12-16)* For those that do not have the spirit of Christ, do not belong to him. *(Romans 8:9)*

Chapter 20

If faith is the substance of hope, why does it fail at times?

How much faith do we have - can it be measured? Strangely enough, the answer to both these questions is a resounding yes. "For by the grace given me I tell everyone among you not to think of himself more highly than one ought to think, but to think soberly, each according to *the measure* of faith that *God has apportioned*." *(Romans 12:3)* The answer to the amount of faith that we have is "the measure." The Greek word for measure is *metron* that means, *a portion taken off*. In fact, you have the same faith as Saint Paul or Saint Peter. You also have the same faith as Saint Teresa of Avila, Saint Francis of Assisi and Saint Thomas Aquinas, Saint Augustine or any of the men and women in the Bible. In fact, you have the same faith as all the great Saints including those in the Bible. The difference is how they responded in faith to get it to the level of sanctity and ability.

Our faith, whilst complete in order for us to believe in God's existence, fails due to a lack of knowledge and right action regarding God's instructions. This can be for several reasons and not the least of which is having no real knowledge of the Bible upon which to act in an effective manner. Consequently, the Logos does not become Rhema in us and there is little or no result. Rather than read the Bible and plumb its depths as the Vatican Council II

Dogmatic Constitution Dei Verbum Chapter 3; 12 encourages us to do, many people build their faith on what others have said without checking it out for themselves. These people tend to skip the surface of the Bible even if they do read it and it is likely that they do not consult a concordance or Bible dictionary to look into either the historical situation or language in which the Bible authors wrote it.

The other problem with faith for most people who struggle and experience great disappointment, is that they do not do what others have done to get their faith to the same level. This is the situation for those who listen to a person of great faith and are inspired by what they hear and often see, and then immediately run out to do similar things.

An example of this is a person that listens to a speaker testifying to the great works they have accomplished in Christ. The speaker tells how God has provided great wealth and success, or how God has used them for miraculous healing or vast numbers of conversions. Inspired by what they hear, the person gives up their well-paid job and decides to live by faith only to be disappointed and crestfallen at their failure. Another goes off and lays their hands on a seriously sick person only to find that they did not recover, and in some cases the person they had prayed for died in spite of what they expected from the accounts they had heard.

By these failures, not only do these people become despondent but also many clergymen are very suspicious of people who speak about faith and some even spurn those who teach it. This is understandable considering the failures they have encountered with people that have believed for a healing and not received it; their pastoral hearts leaps into protect-mode for the sake of the suffering and the disillusioned for whom they have dedicated their lives to love and protect.

Without understanding the nature and law of faith, it will always remain a mystery; we will continue to wonder why some people receive healing and others do not and so we will fall short with encouragement for those who need it. When this happens, the person is usually encouraged to accept their misfortune as God's will and a cross they must bear. The promise of Christ spoken at the great commission, as with all his teaching, does not bear this out. Jesus promises recovery, which indicates clearly that in the ordinary ways of God it takes time. *(Mark 16:18)*

Therefore, it seems expedient that we should persist in faith as Jesus taught until there is no need to persist. If we persist with patience, it will come in its due season. Whatever the outcome we will then live with hope rather than despair, and that everlasting virtue of hope will, by its very nature, brings our mind into a positive condition that will consequently affect the body in a positive way; there is nothing to loose.

When we do this regarding our health we cooperate with the natural healing processes built into the body's immune system by God to function for our health and protection. The natural response in the body to any threat is to kill the invader. The immune system is aggressive in this regard and it is there to keep us healthy and protect us from sickness. It should not seem so strange therefore, that by faith we take the same attitude of mind and cooperate with the natural healing process by accepting that all things are possible for the one who believes.

Why some people receive healing and some do not, will always remain a mystery. However, that should not diminish the effectiveness of divine revelation in these matters for to do so will leave many suffering for no good

137

purpose. In my book, 12 Steps to Divine Healing, it stated that, "What you put your faith in determines what comes out." This remains true in spite of criticism some have levelled at this proposal. This is so because the one believing that he can, and the one believing that he cannot are both correct. However, it seems expedient as we begin to grasp the law and nature of faith that we should err, if we are to err at all, on the side of God's Word being more reliable than our own lived experiences, which more often than not fall short of what God has revealed and expects of us.

Many people have a faith based on their own or others opinions and personal observations rather than faith based on God's promises. Therefore, if a person believes that their unfortunate circumstance is God's will for their benefit, it is reasonable to suppose that they will not seek God's solution and most likely remain in bondage to it. This is the measure of their faith, and it flies in the face of God's abundant mercy for the lost, sick and suffering since there is no evidence in the Gospel, that this should be so.

It is imperative that we do the things that others of faith have done to get our faith to their level in order for us to get the same results. Unless we do this, we will always fail when we try to achieve the same works. Both the Bible and the Church present to us men and women of great faith so that we cannot only aspire to those heights in our daily lives, but moreover to imitate them in order for our faith to grow to that level; faith without works is a dead faith.

Jesus of course, is the one that we should imitate par excellence and it is possible to do so because he tells us that all things are possible for the one who believes. After all, Jesus himself beckons us to follow him on the narrow way of faith through a tiny door that opens wider as we journey along.

Chapter 21

Why is the Bible account regarding healing different from our experience?

There are many reasons why our experience of healing can often differ from what the Bible records and not the least is what I call the Nazarene syndrome in my book 12 Steps to Divine Healing. Matthew records an account of Jesus returning to Nazareth where he was born, but not many received healing from him although he was willing to do so.

After speaking in the synagogue in Nazareth, the people that grew up with him questioned his authority and miracles, and they took offence at him. Consequently, he did not work any mighty deeds there because of their lack of faith.

The Nazarene syndrome is the group of symptoms that caused them to question and doubt. The consequence was that they remained sick even though Jesus was willing and able to heal them. In our days, the problem often remains the same and affected by our personal history. *(Luke 4:14-30)*

All the great saints modelled their lives on Jesus Christ, and we should do the same. However, we notice that many were sick and infirm in spite of their faith and this can cause us to wonder at the apparent contradictions between what the Bible says and what those Saints experienced even though they did not doubt Jesus ability to heal as we see in the miracles recorded in their lives. This of course was a very common situation but there does seem to be a logical reason for it that goes back over many centuries.

During the first centuries before the conversion of the Roman Emperor Constantine, Christians suffered greatly at the hands of the Romans. Commonly this was crucifixion or death in the arenas by lions. During this period immediately after the resurrection, it meant that Christians could expect martyrdom and therefore died as Christ did sharing in his sufferings for the sake of the Gospel.

During that period, the occurrence of healing and miracles recorded in the epistles was normal Christianity as we see in the lives of Peter, John and Paul recorded as apostolic teaching but do we really have that faith that comes to us from those Apostles today?

Some four hundred years afterwards when the Roman Emperor Constantine became a Christian, he declared Christianity the new state religion. Persecution stopped and the pagan Roman Empire became the Holy Roman Empire. Suddenly the tradition of martyrdom to attain heaven was no longer there. As a result, the Christians stopped calling in the presbyters to anoint them for healing. *(James 5:13-18)*

In all likelihood, they began to accept their sickness or misfortune as a way of carrying their cross. This became another way of martyrdom: one that has continued until today even though extreme unction is now in its rightful place and understanding as the sacrament of the anointing of the sick based upon James chapter five.

Suffering with great patience and offering it up for others is a wonderful thing that can, and does, produce holiness. However, this is not the cross Jesus said that we should carry each day in order to follow him. The cross Jesus spoke of was the suffering for the sake of the Gospel, not sickness and disease or every calamity that befalls us. Certainly, it is a good thing to use our sickness and misfortune this way, not as fate, but rather by faith until healing or the answer comes. Even so, this view of suffering, accepted as a cross has prevailed even to this day, and it diminishes faith in God's willingness to heal, protect or provide.

We might wonder at the late Pope John Paul II's suffering Parkinson's disease. Of course, we cannot presume to know his inner motives unless he had revealed them, but in this case, we might keep in mind that the world does not value life anymore; anyone with the Pope's responsibilities and suffering Parkinson's disease, leave their job, often under great pressure from others.

In the euthanasia mentality, people with severe illnesses are to die. In the abortion mentality, those with birth defects are to die before they see life in this world. Pope John Paul's life and suffering flies in the face of this death culture and testifies to the value of life.

The Parkinson's disease from which he suffered is a challenge to the culture of death and demonstrates that there is value in a person even in the face of severe infirmity, and in spite of debilitation, that person can contribute a great deal. It was, in this way, true redemptive suffering and a cross that has a sacrificial purpose beyond one's own needs; one that was a voice and witness giving value to all that suffer, and this is great, and even more so, heroic faith.

For those that want to follow this example, it is wise to keep this in mind, for it is not to be for us the way and only way; it is the exception and not the rule for all sickness and suffering. We know that the Pope received medical treatment to cure and relieve his suffering; he did not refuse treatment and neither did those around him encourage refusal. It is only a question of whether or not God is invoked through prayer to remove the sickness. However, millions prayed to God for Pope John Paul's health every day right up to his death, and rightly so. Such was the witness of John Paul's life that his successor Pope Benedict XVI suspended the five-year period towards Beatification and began the cause for his sainthood within weeks of his death.

Chapter 22

Religious legalism undermines faith

When the Pharisees questioned Jesus about telling people that the truth sets them free, they rejected his teaching and cited Abraham as their source of freedom. This showed their pride and bombast stating that as descendants of Abraham they had, "not been enslaved by anyone."

Jesus points out that anyone who sins becomes a slave of sin. These people relied on the law rather than on faith and they continued the debate with Jesus on the issue. They may well have kept the law as a yardstick with which to bind and control others but this was sinning against the spirit of the law.

When Jesus challenges their stubborn hearts by acknowledging that they are indeed children of Abraham, he exposes their inner intent against him as a citation of their sin that was binding them up. They became even more pedantic when Jesus mentioned God as their Father by insisting that Abraham was their father. Jesus said to them, "If you were Abraham's children, you would be doing the works of Abraham." *(John 8:31-39)*

Now this is very interesting because we know that God considered Abraham righteous because of his faith *(Genesis 15:6)* so it would be easy for us to accept that everything that followed in his life was just that, but Jesus also mentions Abraham's works. It would also be easy for us to dismiss this out of hand.

There are so many people today who say they have faith, but do not do the works that faith demands; They belong to a particular faith *(church or religion)* and they, often like the people of Jesus' time, blindly apply a set of doctrines which they believe in, but do not accomplish in their daily lives.

The following story, taken from Vision College in Sydney NSW sums this up very well. 'One day a truculent man approached George Whitfield, stuck out his chin and said, "You'll never get me to change my faith!" "Oh?" said Whitfield, "Perhaps you will tell me then, just what you believe?" "I believe what my church believes!" He said. "Well, what does your church believe?" "My church believes what I believe!" He said, "Well," said Whitfield, a little exasperated but still trying for a sensible reply, "Will you tell me what you believe?" Then the man declared, "We both believe the same thing!" and promptly strode off.

This particular man clearly had bigotry and prejudice, but he did not have faith. What he mistakenly thought was faith was in fact merely a naïve superstition, a gullible acceptance of what someone else had told him; there was no informed understanding in his belief.' *(Vision College Ltd, Sydney, NSW)*

In addition, many people can give up on what began as exciting ventures in the Lord because the rules and constitutions established for guidance used as laws stifle their spirit and rob their joy. Once this happens people give up and leave. The Holy Spirit, unlike the devil or a legalistic person, is a Spirit of order, not a police officer enforcing the letter of the law and nor is he an accuser for the prosecution. The letter of the law kills, but the spirit of the law gives life.

Chapter 23

Faith: the evidence, the realisation, and the hope

Jesus had told his disciples in Luke 17: 5-6 that even if their faith was only the size of a mustard seed, they could just tell a mulberry tree to be up-rooted and planted in the sea and it would obey them. Jesus offers no explanation and does not elaborate on this. In Matthew 17: 20-21, we see this again. Jesus is adamant about faith and chastises the disciple for the lack of it calling them a perverse generation after they failed to cast a demon from a young boy, "If you have faith the size of a mustard seed, you will say to this mountain, 'Move from here to there,' and it will move. Nothing will be impossible for you."

We have also seen from Hebrews 11:1 that it considers faith as the realisation of hope and evidence of things not seen. It is not surprising therefore that if no discernible effect is experienced after asking God to increase our faith we obviously need to believe without evidence, since faith is the very evidence of itself testifying to the substance of what we are hoping for when we ask for it.

To grasp an insight into this explanation we need to identify some keywords in this verse which are; realisation, hope and evidence. Evidence is present and seen and therefore, it is tangible. The Webster's Dictionary explains evidence as; "that which makes evident or provides a sign or indication of something; that which shows or establishes

145

the truth or falsity of something; proof; testimony; *law,* that which is legally submitted to a competent tribunal as a means of ascertaining the truth of anything under investigation. In evidence; easily seen or noticed."

Let us now paraphrase Hebrews thus far and see what it says, 'Faith is the sign which shows forth and establishes the truth which is easily seen and noticed as proof.' Faith therefore is its own evidence, and it is sufficient as the very proof of what we believe and what we are hoping for in order to see a desired result. Never the less, faith is not a blind force based on an empty hope; rather, faith is based on something totally reliable, unfading and secure. That security and certainty is simply, a promise. Activated and owned in the now, a promise makes the future present to us. If we believe a promise then we have something to look forward to and something to live for. This is the substance of hope; it makes what is yet to come present to us and it makes sense of what Jesus meant when he said, "Be as though you have received."

The Christian virtue of hope is not a vain thing. Saint Paul tells us that hope is one of the three things that last, "Faith, hope and love." *(1Corintians 13:13)* Unlike a worldly concept, Christian hope is to have our minds filled with a confident expectation of everything that is good and it is especially, although not specifically, directly associated with God's promise of salvation; it is reliable because God is faithful to his promise.

Ephesians 6:17, says that hope is a "helmet of salvation." It is interesting to note that Saint Paul places salvation on the head as a protective helmet. This is because our mind is the battleground that Satan attacks. In Eden, the serpent does not so much cause Adam and Eve to hate God, but by his subtle distortions of what God had said, he causes them to forget about God. By focusing their attention on the forbidden tree until it begins to look good does this very effectively and he still works this way today.

Distracted by the serpent's distorted argument, Adam and Eve lost faith in what God had said to them. The result was the fall and fear was the consequence; they had now put their faith in what the serpent had said and that resulted in fear and death. Fear is the opposite of faith and death is the consequence of losing hope. The virtue of Christian hope therefore, is to fill our mind with a confident expectation of everything that is good concerning what God has said regarding our salvation and wellbeing.

What we believe is what we put our faith in, and what we put our faith in determines the result; this is an activity of the mind and the subsequent free-will choices that we make. It is the liberation of the mind that sets us free to act rightly and therefore people, holy angels and evil angels can also present ideas and images to our minds and what we choose to entertain in our thoughts inevitably becomes an action in our lives.

The hope of our salvation is available immediately on acceptance of Jesus by faith according to what we hear, and it guarantees the future fulfilment through his promises received in the present. *(Romans 10:17)* In Ephesians, 6:17 Saint Paul says that the helmet is the hope of our salvation. In other words, it is an attitude of mind in confident expectation of everything good coming to us as God has promised. This gives us peace of mind. The helmet protects the head so that the hope we entertain is safe from doubt and fear. Saint Paul also tells us that the battleground is the human mind and that we bring every thought captive in obedience with Christ. *(2Corinthians 3-5, 2Corinthians 10:3-6, Ephesians 3:23.)*

Chapter 24

A childlike faith lost in the vagary of adulthood

*T*hroughout your life you have experienced faith albeit not necessarily faith in God. This is because everyone is born with faith and you have not only exercised it, but you have seen the tangible proof and touched the very thing that you hoped for by faith many times.

Think back a moment to your childhood. Do you remember your parents asking what you wanted for Christmas? Do you remember what you asked for? Were you vague or were you precise? The chances are that you were very precise; if it was a doll, you said exactly what doll you wanted and described it by name and in precise detail and, most likely told your parents or Santa where they could purchase it. If it was a skateboard or computer game, you did exactly the same thing. Do you remember your parents saying that if you were good, Santa would bring it for you? Well, if you are like any other normal person you certainly do.

Do you remember lying awake at night worrying yourself silly, wondering if you could really believe what your parents said, or did you fall asleep while playing with the toy in your imagination? Again, the chances are that the latter was true. Even though your parents used the word 'if', you did not because for you there were no ifs or buts about it; as far as you were concerned, it was a foregone conclusion and an absolute fact. Do you remember feeling fulfilled, excited, and telling your friends what you were getting for Christmas even though it was probably several months away?

If this was so, you were experiencing expectant faith. The Greek for *expect* or *expectation* is *apokaradokia* and means, a watching with outstretched head. It signifies strained expectancy, eager longing, the stretching forth of the head indicating and expectation of something from a certain place. *(Romans 8:9. Philippians 1:20)*

A clearer understanding comes from the Greek construction of the word *apokaradokia*. *Apo,* meaning abstraction and absorption - abstraction from anything that might engage the attention and absorption in the object expected until the fulfilment is realised, *kara;* the head and *dokeo;* to look or to watch. Faith; Greek, *pistis;* a firm persuasion or conviction based on hearing. *(Romans 10:17)*

The promise made long before Christmas Day gave you something to look forward to and it gave you something to live for each successive day; this is the substance of hope and the evidence of what you cannot see, and the only time you lost sleep was on Christmas Eve. This was because the promised gift was imminent. You lost sleep because you were excited in anticipation of finally seeing the promise the next morning and not because you were worrying yourself sick.

Not only could you not sleep due to your excitement, but you also arose very early and fully alert, much to the consternation of your parents. Finally, there it is under the Christmas tree. However, could you see it? No, you could only see the wrapping; the bright coloured paper was only a tangible sign and an outward expression of the promised, but still yet, unseen gift.

After sorting through every parcel under the tree, ignoring all that did not mention you, you finally find your name, and shredding the neatly wrapped paper with impatient abandon, life and joy ignited your soul and delight filled your mind as you discovered that the promise was true! Now, and only now, the promised gift is right there revealed to your physical eyes and touched with the physical body and at that very moment, nothing else seemed to exist, except that precious gift.

What happened? When did we grow up? When did we get the idea that we needed to see in order to believe and posses to own the promise? When did we loose that childlike faith of which is the very substance of what we hoped for and the delight and pleasure of our Heavenly Father as well as our own? When did we shut the door on the Kingdom of God? Could it be when we became mature? That being the case, we have to ask ourselves why our faith did not mature along with us.

To discover the answer, we need to ask when we actually possessed the gift. Most people would say that it was on Christmas Day when we tore off the wrapping paper. However, at the time of the promise, the gift was present to us and that is when we possessed it. We can know this to be so because that is when we first began to play with the promised gift.

When could we see the gift so that we could believe? Again, most people would say on Christmas Day, but the truth is that we could see it the moment that we accepted the promise. This is so because we believed what we had heard, trusted the one who said it and played with the gift in our mind every night and sometimes throughout the day until it arrived. Christmas Day was the season for its manifestation into the physical world when the spoken promise had achieved its purpose and happened.

Therefore, faith based on a promise is the guarantee and the future realized in the present, and you have been experiencing it naturally all your life because the ability to do so was there the day you were born. However, the ability to put your faith in Jesus Christ is a gift of grace from God that also comes from hearing a promise.

This is borne out when Jesus asks his disciples who do people say he is. There are several responses; Elijah, John the Baptist, one of the Prophets returned from the dead, but Jesus asks, "But who do you say I am?" Simon responds that he is the Christ, the Son of the Living God. Jesus tells Simon, "It is not flesh and blood that has revealed this to you, but my Father in heaven."

Jesus then tells Simon that he was henceforth to have the name Peter (Greek; Petra) meaning Rock, and that upon that Rock Jesus would build his Church. The Rock was the grace of faith given through revelation by God to Simon to believe that Jesus is truly Lord and Christ.

The ability to believe this with the complete trust and acceptance of a child believing a parent for a gift is the substance of the virtue of what Jesus says, "Lest your faith be that of a little child, you cannot enter the Kingdom of God." The rock is also Peter himself who becomes the leader of the Apostles after Jesus ascended into heaven and sent the Holy Spirit at Pentecost.

Jesus is not vague about childlike faith. Throughout Jesus' ministry he would often say, "Go, your faith has healed you." It is our faith placed in the promises that God has made that gives us hope until what we believe for comes to us; justified in what we have believed we see the result. By faith, Abraham received the power to have children, even though he was past the normal age and Sarah was sterile, "for he thought that the one who had made the promise was trustworthy." (Hebrews 11:11)

God's promises are far more reliable than that of a friend or a parent no matter how sincere they might be. God cannot break a promise because according to covenant law he must by that very law come under the curse of the law and destroy himself if he did so, which he cannot do. In addition, God's love for his children forbids him to renege on a promise he has made. Therefore, God's promises are reliable and we can trust them no matter what the circumstances dictate.

When we believe with the simplicity of a child trusting a parent for a gift, we will recover our innocence and, pleasing God; we will receive what he has promised. Faith pleases God just as a trusting child pleases a parent; the parent finds joy in seeing the child excited and grateful even though they cannot see the gift and the parent shares in the excitement as their joy builds to see the happiness on the face of their children on Christmas morning.

For us this means receiving the Kingdom of God in the same way, and through this pure heart, we will see God and the beauty of his Kingdom. In addition, we will inherit all that the Kingdom of God contains including God himself from the position of a first-born son, and all this by simply believing what the Bible has said about our redemption by the blood of Jesus Christ.

My late father who was a great optimist had said that a pessimist was like a man who wore braces as well as a belt to hold up his trousers. It seems he understood the difference between having faith and lacking it. Clearly faith is not a superstitious magic incantation or a kind of cure all, solve all formula chanted to force our will upon a given situation. For in fact, faith forces nothing and no one, it simply believes and trusts that God will act in our best interest even if we do not know what that best interest is.

Several years ago whilst taking Holy Communion to a young lady suffering from severe cerebral palsy the family would plead that I pray for her healing, which I did every week after communion. Their desperation had caused them to seek all sorts of New Age cures even from psychic healers in the Philippines. After some time I became frustrated seeing no apparent result and feeling the pressure from the family I prayed for God to reveal why no healing seemed evident.

God showed that he could heal in an instant and asked if I understood all the ramifications of such a miracle; had I taken into account the effect this would have on my family as well as theirs. Many things paraded before my mind's eyes as though peering into the future and I understood that God takes everything and everyone into account before he acts. At this, I left the outcome to him and continued to pray for healing.

It was some months later that the mother began to tell of the changes in her daughter. She had been very intelligent as a child but had given up hope of achieving anything, refused an education and had become very bitter. Due to the prayer and the affirmations that she received each Sunday, she began to take an interest in her education once more. She learned to read and write even though it was by holding the instrument in her mouth. In addition, she became more joyful and the former bitterness vanished.

When attending the institute with her fellow sufferers her constant complaining turned to encouragement and praying with them to achieve their potential in spite of their infirmities. This had a beneficial impact at the hospital including the staff and the patients expressing more joy each day as they looked forward to achieving something worthwhile.

Upon hearing this, I understood that God had taken all into account in his own good time. Had he healed this young woman instantly as the family and I had been asking, the others could have felt even more rejected and worthless and the resulting jealousy would have made them even more bitter increasing their sad state. However, when seeing what one of the worst suffers could achieve it inspired them to achieve too.

The wonderful thing is that throughout this process, my young communicant gradually gained more physical mobility and control over her body and this was evident for all to see; God had turned a bitter young woman who had given up hope into a loving inspiration to others.

Whichever way God chooses to work, we must of necessity, trust him with the outcome in his good time without loosing hope or faith in what he has promised. Just because we could not see what we desired at the time, it did not mean that God had not heard our prayers or was not working in the situation. Clearly, due to bitterness and the constant dabbling with alternative occult remedies God could not act until these attitudes had changed.

Once they began to put their faith in Jesus, Jesus acted and the healing process began. Christmas was now better than before because my young friend was able to open her presents by her own efforts for the first time. Therefore, "Let us hold unwaveringly to our confession that gives us hope, for he who made the promise is trustworthy." *(Hebrews 10:23)*

Chapter 25

Faith heals us of worry

Jesus said, "If one of your children asked you for fish, would you give them a snake, or if they asked you for bread would you give them a stone? Well, if you who are full of sin know how to give your children what is good, how much more will your heavenly Father give you who ask him, O you of little faith." *(Matthew 7:7-11)* Jesus is saying that God has promised to meet our needs in every area of our daily life and we can put our faith and trust in what he has said regarding it, "Therefore I tell you not to worry about your life."

Worry is a consequence of doubt and fear and in this case, it is the fear that we will not have enough provision for the future. Worry is another word for fear, and fear is perverted faith; in fact, fear is the opposite of faith. Because fear cannot see the outcome, it causes us to worry, despair, and become anxious about many things, especially the things we cannot change such as the past or the future and consequently it robs us of all the opportunities in the present.

Often the consequence of worry, even about small things, can result in many forms of sickness. The reason is that fear and worry debilitates and weakens, like a wolf worrying sheep debilitating them before he attacks. It is the same when worry causes us to be sick physically as well as emotionally; our immune system eventually looses resistance and we become defenceless against diseases. Worry will also make us inefficient in dealing with daily tensions. In addition, the effects of worry and fear on our nervous system can increase our heart rate and bring on palpitations thus increasing anxiety and even heart problems.

This nervous tension can also cause such irritability and stress that it affects our ability to digest food and the tension can increase stomach acids as well as a loss of appetite. Eventually the lack of food or poor diet, poor digestion and increased stomach acids can burn holes in the stomach lining and nervous tension, anxiety and worry cause skin irritations as well as many other conditions.

All these things debilitate the body's natural function causing physical breakdown and so our mental anguish is increased. It can cause us to be irritable with other people, saying or doing things that we regret; we cannot concentrate on our work, we become more inefficient and thus the worry and anxiety is increased and we begin to dislike ourselves and become regretful.

In our relationships, it can bring sexual dysfunction causing tension between spouses, the list could go on, and on; when unabated, worry and fear can become an ever-descending spiral dragging us into severe depression and in the extreme; the loss of hope causes suicide.

Many people, especially mother's, think they do not love someone if they do not worry about them, most especially their children. The truth is that worry is not an act of loving. On the contrary, it causes the worrier to consternate over many little things and they can become overbearing, controlling, angry, and demanding. All of which drives their children into frustration and rebellion, thus increasing worry. In other words, it is self-defeating and increases insecurity and it harms and destroys others into the bargain.

Quyen is a young woman that attended our 2004 Congress called, *A Summertime of Grace - Receiving the Mercy of God.* Compulsive behaviour, worry, and stress, made her a prisoner to fear. "I was a captive; a captive of my unnecessary worry and anxieties and knew I had to break the chains of bondage to stress. Stress was seriously debilitating me physically, mentally and emotionally; I was always feeling unwell, lethargic and sometimes had trouble breathing because I was so tense."

Quyen suffered rapid weight loss due to her stress and could not sleep at night. "I was so anxious I could not sleep and so I would clean my house concerned that I was not spending my time efficiently and productively; I would not allow myself to rest until I had meticulously organised and planned what I was going to do for each day of the week."

At 2am, she would compulsively and repeatedly, ensure that the alarm clock was set for 5.30am. "It was all a complete waste of time because I rarely ever got out of bed at 5.30am, not out of laziness, but because I would spend the next two to three hours worried and analysing what might go wrong if I commenced my day; my neurotic thoughts were paralysing me mentally and emotionally."

These preoccupations caused social debilitation and caused her to run from social interactions. She would force herself to mingle for ten to twenty minutes but felt extremely distressed because, "I had no sanctuary or place to hide from my friends! I just wanted to go home because I was close to bursting into tears."

At the Congress Quyen plucked up the courage to go for prayer in order to be free from this debilitating compulsive disorder. "I wanted to ask for the emotional

157

healing my heart desired but my feet seemed glued to the floor and would not let me. I did not know why I felt like this but I realised I was allowing the devil to play on my weakness and anxiety. It was pathetic and I felt pathetic; how could my anxiety be set free if I was anxious about going for prayer? I was anxious about being anxious."

After a struggling in fear, she finally responded in faith to Jesus' call to begin a new life in him, "I was yearning to have a brand new heart, and when Eddie made the altar call he asked the delegates if they wanted to die to self and accept Jesus that night. My answer was an emphatic yes!, because I knew I had to let myself die to myself as I was so that I could become a brand new creature in Christ - I don't want this anymore!"

As prayer for her liberty began, Quyen burst into tears and when asked to surrender to the Lord, Jesus touched her, "Instantly I felt wobbly, but I subconsciously resisted falling. Kay advised that I should yield to God and when I did, I fell to the floor. For the first time, I was lying on the floor paralysed by the Holy Spirit. It was such a peaceful moment lying there oblivious to everything else going on.

When I managed to get up my legs felt like jelly and my heart was beating rapidly. After a while, I felt a sharp pain in my chest, my heart hurt but it was a 'good hurt'. Instead of God just filling the hole in my heart, he reached inside and gave me a heart transplant."

Quyen began to cry with gratitude to God, "But these were not the sad tears of bottled up unresolved childhood problems, or the weary tears of a young woman who recently felt close to having a mental breakdown. I was free and liberated because I was saved by the grace and mercy of a loving almighty Father. I cried tears of joy for the first time in my life and I did not have a heavy and burdened heart anymore. I was no longer a captive because the chains of bondage to stress are broken. Jesus had set me free indeed! I felt light as a feather and an immense wave of joy flooded my heart and body. It overflowed and I praised God in a way that I had never praised before.

That night with the grace of God, I overcame my anxieties and so I sang and danced for joy praising our Heavenly Father I know I am healed emotionally and I thank God for this. God has worked so many miracles in my life and I know he will continue to do so. I also know that sometimes I will worry and stress but it will never again cause me to be so debilitated or make me a captive with a heavy heart again."

Quyen's story shows that Jesus offers a reason to have faith by assuring us that God knows exactly what we need. He tells us that worry cannot achieve anything good and no matter how much we worry, it will not add one millisecond to our span of life; on the contrary, it will diminish it as Quyen has testified in her young life. Jesus is teaching us to have our faith in Yahweh Yireh, a title that means, "God's provision will be seen."

Jesus gives the secret to faith in God's provision when he says, "Seek first the Kingdom of God and his righteousness, and all things will be given to you besides. Do not worry about tomorrow; tomorrow will take care of its self. Sufficient for a day is its own evil." *(Matthew 6: 25-34)* Therefore, the three-step formula to our provision is, *(1)* seek the Kingdom. *(2)* seek his righteousness and *(3)* cast your cares upon him because he cares for you. *(1Peter 5:7)*

Chapter 26

Cast you cares on Jesus and receive bread from heaven

In Luke 11:5-8 Jesus tells a parable about a man who had a visitor late at night. He had no food to give him and so he went to a friend's house. Arriving at his friend's house, he knocked on the door but there was no answer. He knocked again and still there was no answer. Undeterred he kept knocking. Finally, a bleary-eyed neighbour appeared at the upper window, "Who's there? What do you want?"

The man told him about a visitor arriving late and asked if he would give him a loaf of bread. The man refused him saying that it was late, everyone is in bed and the door locked for the night, so he could not give him the bread. Jesus then said, "I tell you truly, if friendship doesn't cause him to get up and give him the bread, persistence surely will."

This parable reveals many things about prayer and the answers we seek as well as how faith works. First, the man recognised his need in what he was lacking. He was specific about what he needed and exactly when he needed it. He went to the source of supply; presented that need to his friend and he kept persisting until the bread he had asked for was is in his hand.

It is reasonable to assume that Jesus means us to understand that the man had heard in some manner that his friend had bread. This being the case, he acted on what he had heard, believed it and asked for what he needed and persisted until it came.

He could not see the bread at any time; his only evidence was to believe by what he had heard until it came to him. Jesus is showing us that what could not be seen with the physical eyes eventually becomes manifest in our physical presence in its due season. This happens by having faith in what is promised, believing it will happen, being specific about what we need and persisting until it comes. This parable gives four keys to receiving answers to prayer: Believe. Have faith. Be specific. Persist.

In other words, Jesus is teaching us that God has made the promises and those promises are complete and reliable. We cannot see what he has promised with our physical eyes and so we must believe what he has said until we do; our faith as a seed planted in the rich soil of God's promises brings forth the harvest of the Word in its due season and gives us reason not to worry.

Cast your cares *(worries)* upon him, because he cares for you. *(1Peter 5:7)* To cast means to smash to the ground with force, so Saint Peter speaks plainly regarding our attitude to dealing with our cares. We can do this only by faith, believing that what God has promised to us in his Word will happen for us. When we do trust God by faith, our days go by without unnecessary worry; it lets us see better the opportunities for every good that God has placed in our path. The consequence is peace of mind; that elusive condition of soul that we often ask God to give but never seemingly achieve. "Stress is trying to change what we cannot change, whereas the secret of our future lies in the ordinary things of our daily life." *(Mike Murdoch)*

The opportunity to ignite the moment is always there because God and his Word never changes; God's Word is reliable and we can put out total trust in it.

Whatever is in your life right now is the sum total of your past, what you decide to do with it now will determine the future. Jesus is teaching us to be specific; if we want bread ask for bread and not just something to eat. Therefore, we are to ask him believing that we will receive what we ask for according to his promises and persist in faith until we receive it, but most importantly, we are to be specific about what we ask because we will get what you ask for.

Saint James says that we do not receive what we ask because we ask wrongly. *(James 4:1-3)* He says that to pray wrongly is when we want something just for our whim and therefore it is wasted. To pray rightly is to pray according to the Word of God, that is, according to his will as revealed in Scripture, expressing a real need. In the parable of the man and the bread, Jesus is telling us how to pray in the right way and thus receive what we ask.

For example, a friend tells you that he would give you whatever you asked to eat or drink the next time you visited his home, and so you have two choices, believe or not believe what he has promised. Of course, if you do not believe then you will either not go to his home at all, and if you did, you would not ask him for something to eat or drink, in which case you have received according to your faith; nothing. No faith means you go nowhere and get nothing as a result.

Alternatively, you decide to take him at his word and pay him a visit. On your arrival, he asks what you would like, and so you say you would like something to eat and drink. A short while later he returns with a cheese sandwich with pickle sauce, which you hate, and glass of sour grape juice, which you detest. Did you get what you asked for? Yes, of course you did. How is that you might ask. Well, you got exactly what you said, "something" to eat and "something" to drink. Your meal arrived according as your faith had spoken.

However, let us suppose that on your arrival, your appetite needed a cup of coffee and a ham sandwich and so you told your friend exactly what you needed. Surely, according to what he promised to you he would return with exactly what you asked for. Now, rather than disappointment and embarrassment, you have joy and satisfaction; your appetite is filled and your friend seems more reliable than you might have thought and you are rewarded with a grateful heart; the atmosphere of friendship grows ever deeper and your faith begins to grow as a result.

Jesus says that he calls us friends. The promises of our friend Jesus are in heaven; the supernatural realm of God. The promise not seen with the natural eyes, as with the man needing the bread could not see the bread from outside the door, is available to us by asking in faith; our faith in God's Word makes God's provision in the supernatural known in the natural realm of human knowledge and reason where we can posses it fully.

The Holy Spirit, whose role is to reveal the mind of God and to glorify the Son reveals the revelations of God's promises. Jesus said that he only did and spoke that which his Father had revealed to him.

In other words, faith is taking God seriously at his Word so that what is ours in the supernatural is released to us in the natural just as the ham sandwich and the coffee was received and that gift became manifest at Christmas some time after the promise was made. We ask according to his will and not our whims, "Your will be done on earth as it is in heaven. Give us this day our daily bread..."

In other words, the things we need today are secured in the promises of God in heaven made manifest on earth for our good and provision along with everything that pertains to our eternal salvation beginning right here in the ordinary events of our daily life. Therefore, have faith and do not worry. God really does care for you.

Chapter 27

Faith saves the guilty and grants mercy

Some years ago, shortly after a profound conversion experience, I was witnessing to Jesus in pubs and clubs. On one occasion, attacked by three bouncers, my ankle was shattered with a karate blow and my body beaten so severely I spent over a month in hospital and my wounds took over eight months to heal. A street fighter as a youth, this was the first time that I did not want revenge or retribution. As I fell to the ground, I prayed and forgave them before I passed out under the blows of fists and boots.

Many wonderful things by the grace of God happened while I was in hospital even to experiencing divine union. I did wonder why this and many other things had happened; some of my clients rejected my graphic arts business and I lost major accounts because of my faith in Jesus, and so I asked God about it. The answer he gave was, "When a man hears the truth he sees the light, but the light hurts his eyes, so he attacks the truth."

After pondering his answer, it became clear that our eyes are to receive light, but when we enter a dark room, we feel no pain. After some time in the dark, our eyes adjust and when the light switch ignites the globe, the light hurts our eyes and we block out the light. If it is severe, we can even get angry at the light. It is the same with sin. Created in the image of God, we are to receive his light and reflect his glory; this is our natural state.

165

When we enter sin, we feel no pain. After a time we become accustomed to it and it appears to be normal, that is until the truth comes. It is then that we experience pain, reject the truth, and attack the one who presented it to us in spite of the fact that we, created for truth as our natural human function, should welcome it. In the case of the three bouncers, this light had activated a violent reaction.

However, for me it was not a matter of exacting retribution and punitive damages under law for their crime, which they did in all justice, deserve, but of praying for their conversion in the spirit of God's hesed *(mercy)* for God's justice is in fact, his mercy. Jesus highlights this in the beatitudes, "Blessed are the merciful for they shall receive mercy." *(Matthew 5:7)*

Friends and others naturally ridiculed my response to what was clearly a vicious attack, but it did not deter the resolve made, because if they were convicted of a crime it would accomplish no great benefit except to harden their hearts and eventually give them something to boast about within their peer groups. Because I was on God's business when this happened, I trusted God to take care of it. My prayer was that they would see the error of their ways, accept Jesus, and change their lives for the good without the stain of a criminal record.

I suffered ridicule and accusations of irresponsibility for over a year. I did not dispute the argument put forward that if I did not press charges others could also suffer the same fate. Despite this, although faith seems irrational and certainly, an enigmatic paradox, I knew that God does not want the death of the sinner but that he repents and lives.

A year later, I witnessed the justification of my faith. A client who owned an advertising agency had found faith in Jesus around the same time as me. He became a

Pentecostal and later, a pastor. On that occasion, I attended his ordination. After the service, people gave each other a greeting.

As I turned around, I received a very warm hug from a very large man and as our eyes met, I recognised him and he recognised me. For a moment, we just looked at each other and then tears welled up in his eyes as he apologised and asked forgiveness – he was the bouncer that had shattered my ankle. Indescribable joy filled me and such gratitude to God overcame me that I nearly fainted.

I then discovered that after the bashing, he had met a young woman and through her influence, he gave his life to Jesus. He was so much in love with God, that at the mere mention of the name Jesus he would fall to floor. Due to this love of Christ, his Pentecostal brethren had nicknamed him, "Canvas Back."

Some time later, I was without a car and had to travel by bus. One night I was working late and did not get my usual connection. When the bus arrived, I paid the driver and recognised him as one of the other bouncers. Although I suspected he recognised me I said nothing and took my seat.

During the forty-five minute journey, many things railed through my mind, but I prayed for God's grace to be able to forgive once more, what seemed to be an unrepentant sinner. Arriving at my destination, I had to pass the driver and began to alight. Taking courage, I turned back and said, "Excuse me, but I think I know you." He replied, "I know you too." Asking if he was one of the bouncers, his embarrassment glowed on his face. I asked how he was doing and put out my hand in friendship to him.

That friendly gesture relaxed him and triggered a response. He related how, shortly after the beating, he had suffered some distressing misfortune. His new girlfriend told him about Jesus and he gave his life to Christ. He was now married and had a child. He was excited to talk about his family saying they attended church every week together and then unexpectedly, he asked for forgiveness. Well, this time I nearly fell off the bus, but I was glad I avoided that because a pavement is harder than carpet and I would not want the nickname, "Concrete Back." I happily forgave him, shook hands, and we parted as friends thanking God for his grace and mercy.

I do not know what happened to the third bouncer but I have no doubt in my mind that if God can get two out of three, he can get three. The two screws that are still in my ankle are a reminder to pray for the other bouncer and I will continue to do so until hearing the good news about him too. The blessing of not knowing anything about him is that he is getting a lot of prayer and blessing from his victim and even a mention in his book, and I am receiving blessings from God for loving my enemies.

The other two tough men had met a gentle man named Jesus. With gentleness so powerful, it overcame the strongman, and his message softened their hearts. I can hazard a guess that they are now bouncers for Jesus beating up Satan rather than people. The light pierced the darkness of their hearts and they have become brand new creatures. Instead of reflecting the savagery of violence, they now reflect the peace of Christ.

When we lift up the Name of Jesus rather than lifting up a fist or retribution, we are justified by faith and victorious in battle. The devil will not fight Jesus again and so we can be sure that he will back off when he sees the light of our faith; a light that the darkness cannot overcome no matter how small it is. As someone once said, "It is impossible for the devil to get anywhere with a grateful heart."

Jesus had forgiven me and showed mercy when I was his enemy, so could I do less than the Master did for me and in whom I now have faith, because for me this is a great cause for gratitude and the substance of my praise. It also reinforces faith in God's ways of justice and mercy rather than in man's, for as previously stated; God's justice is his mercy and has far better results than vengeance.

It is certain that after reading this some will argue that these bouncers deserved police arrest. If so, consider that their lives thus ruined would not have met the spouses that played a crucial role in their change of life and conversion. If incarceration is to bring correction that offenders do no more harm, then forgiveness and mercy accomplished that far more beneficially, most particularly since heartfelt remorse is part of that process. Moreover, how would we feel if after forgiving our sins, Jesus said that we would still have to pay and go to hell?

I did not know how these men had turned out until our meeting, but when Canvas Back wept with sorrow and pain in his heart for what he had done, it seemed right regarding him, as with the bus driver, to say as Jesus did, "Because of their great love, their many sins are forgiven." (Luke 7:47) The power to forgive was present, and when spoken, it brought happiness, liberty, peace, and great joy to all concerned. Whilst it is true that we do not live in an ideal world, we cannot live in a world without ideals.

Chapter 28

The great miracle is not that man can speak to God, but that God speaks to man

*C*ontrary to some popular teaching, especially that emphasised by the meditation movements, God's ordinary way of communicating with man is audibly. Not only are there numerous references to this in the Bible, but also many people hear God when he speaks to them. They do not hear voices in the human sense, but hear God in their spirit with such clarity that it appears to be audible to the ear. Those who experience this can quote exactly what God has said and have a certainly that goes beyond a normal confidence or conviction.

A case in point is God's answer regarding people rejecting his truth as stated previously. In Biblical terms, this is revelation in the same way that Simon knew that Jesus was the Christ. Jesus said flesh and blood had not revealed this to Simon, but his Father in heaven. John the Baptist also heard God speak when he baptised Jesus, but others present at the time do not hear this in the same way if at all.

Jesus is God made man, through Jesus, the Father spoke audibly, and we have a record of what he said in the Bible. After Pentecost, the Holy Spirit imparted through human beings what he wanted people to know by way of the charismatic gift of prophecy and the other utterance gifts: the word of knowledge, the word of wisdom, tongues and the interpretation of tongues recorded in 1Corinthians 12:1-11. All these utterances are to build faith in the hearers and they, by the Holy Spirit, reveal the mind of God who wishes to speak to his children in a way they can understand through the agency of their physical ears in order to convince the soul and reach their spirit.

The other ordinary way that God speaks is through the inspired preaching of the Word. Inspired preaching is the important point here because many simply impart information. Of course, the information imparted if true will inspire acceptance by the soul and will become part of the belief system, but a message inspired by the Holy Spirit brings an experiential conviction that affects a direct change of lifestyle and a vigorous, active, living faith that entertains no doubts.

Whether the speaker operates as a teacher, a preacher, or an evangelist, the faith and conviction of the speaker carries the power of the Spirit and so the message is clearly understood. In other words, we are effective depending on our own belief. This means that if a person is speaking of going to heaven but does not have a firm conviction of their own salvation, their message will be ineffectual. "I believe, therefore, I spoke." *(Psalm 116:10)* This applies to all matters of faith. If you believe it, speak it; speaking will turn it into a reality.

Faith is the spiritual dimension of man. It activates all his activities for good or bad depending on and in what he has placed his faith. God who is Spirit speaks to us in a spiritual language fully understood only in the soul through our spirit. Those that are living their lives at the level of the flesh or of the soul cannot grasp this unless convinced by hearing the Word of God. In 1Corinthians chapter two, Saint Paul makes this very clear. "When I came to you, brothers, proclaiming the mystery of God, I did not come with sublimity of words or of wisdom, for I resolved to know nothing while I was with you except Jesus Christ, and him crucified. I came to you in weakness, fear, and much trembling, and my message and my proclamation were not with persuasive words of wisdom, but with a demonstration of spirit and power, so that your faith might rest not on human wisdom but on the power of God.

Yet, we do speak wisdom to those that are mature, but not wisdom of this age, or of the rulers of this age who are passing away. Rather we speak of God's wisdom, mysterious, hidden, which God predetermined before the ages for his glory, and which none of the rulers of this age knew, for if they had known it, they would not have crucified the Lord of glory. But it is written: 'What eye has not seen, and ear has not heard, and what has not entered the human heart, what God has prepared for those that love him,' to this God has revealed to us through the Spirit.

For the Spirit scrutinises everything, even the depths of God. Among human beings, who can know what pertains to a person except the spirit of that person that is within? Similarly, no one knows what pertains to God except the Spirit of God. We have not received the spirit of the world but the Spirit of God, so that we may understand the things freely given us by God. Moreover, we speak about them not with words taught by human wisdom, but with words taught by the Spirit, describing spiritual realities in spiritual terms.

Now the natural person does not accept what pertains to the Spirit of God, for to him it is foolishness, and he cannot understand it, because it is judged spiritually. The spiritual person however, can judge everything, but is not subject to judgment by anyone. For 'who has known the mind of the Lord, so as to counsel him?' But we have the mind of Christ."

The faith we are referring to is the evidence of what we cannot see. It can only become supernatural faith through a supernaturally spoken word; this word once spoken must also, be heard. "Thus faith comes from what is heard, and what is heard comes through the word of Christ." *(Romans 10:17)* Therefore, faith speaks, sees, acts, and gets results.

Apart from answered prayer, a major result is that man turns his eyes from faith in the created heavenly bodies and puts his faith in its Creator instead. Supernatural faith transcends all human knowledge and reveals the knowledge of God, and indeed that of the entire universe.

By the faith-inspired knowledge of God we understand that the universe exists by the Word of God so that what is visible came into being through the invisible and no further evidence is necessary in order to believe it. *(Hebrews 11:3)* For example, before knowing Christ, it could be important to have proof that Noah's Ark existed, but when faith in God's Word comes, evidence for its existence is no longer important, and whether there was proof or not, or even if it ever existed at all, would be of little consequence when faith is present. Such is the transcending power of faith as its own evidence.

Chapter 29

Your word is the measure of your faith

A s with God's Word, so it is with ours. Isaiah 55: 11 says, "So shall my word be that goes forth from my mouth; it shall not return to me void, but shall do my will, achieving the end for which I sent it." Because of the divine image, although distorted through sin, our words have the same effect either for good or for bad regardless of whether we mean the words or not. Jesus speaks plainly and he expects us to do the same for our justification.

He tells us in Matthew 12:33-37, "Either declare the tree good and its fruits good, or declare the tree rotten and its fruit rotten, for a tree is known by its fruit. You brood of vipers, how can you say good things when you are evil? From the fullness of the heart the mouth speaks. A good person brings forth what is good out of a store of goodness, but an evil person brings forth evil from a store of evil. I tell you, on the day of Judgment, people will render an account for every careless word they speak and by your words you will be acquitted and by your words you will be condemned."

That is a very powerful statement. It has even more emphasis when Jesus said that it is not what goes into our mouth that defiles us, but what comes out. This is because what goes into the mouth passes to the stomach, to the bowel and then to the toilet, but what comes out of our mouth comes from the heart and, where our heart is, there is our treasure also, and out of the mouth, the heart speaks. *(Luke 6:45)*

How many people have jokingly said that they might not get a job and later returned home a successful failure; amazingly, we can be more right and confident about being wrong and failing than we can about being right and succeeding. Of course, other factors may also bring failure, but if we enter an interview in this negative mind-set, we act and speak without confidence.

How many times have you said something like that jokingly and a little while later began to have doubts, whereas before you made the joke, you were confident? The chances are that once doubt entered the equation you gave up and did not continue with your original plan or idea. The amazing thing is that neither viewpoint had any hard evidence at the time that either was possible, but we acted, and therefore achieved what we believed.

Remember the words we speak from our mouth go into our ear and into our mind. This is the same with what we think. What we accept in our mind goes into our subconscious and what is in the subconscious becomes our faith expressed in speech and deed for good or bad. It is clear that a parent constantly telling a child that they are stupid will cause that child to speak and act in a stupid way; the child then acting in such a way accepts it as evidence that the words spoken are true and concludes that they really are stupid. In the same way, when we keep telling ourselves that we can, we will, and when we keep telling ourselves that we cannot, we will not; we get what we say. As a man thinks, so he is.

Those with a negative sense of humour are dancing with fire and in danger of fulfilling what they say even though they are joking. Their hearers might catch on to the negative joke and even laugh, but not all of them will. Taken

175

seriously those words can have a devastating result: whilst the conscious mind understands the joke, the subconscious mind, which does not have a sense of humour, does not understand and receives the joke as a fact and consequently impels us subconsciously to act accordingly. As a result, we cannot understand why we act in a certain way when we intended another. The fruit is frustration and a lack of confidence that only perpetuates the cycle of failure: habitual negative humour not only has a negative effect on other people, but also inevitably has a negative effect on the one using it.

What we are and what we say is often a product of learned responses or reactions that have been inbuilt since childhood. Saint Thomas Aquinas teaches that our natural tendency is towards the good and it is under the appearance of good that we are deceived. Examples of this are people that find themselves in difficult situations and turn to lies to save themselves. Lying is wrong, but it appears to be a good way to get out of a problem. People that do not adjust this will become habitual or pathological liars and the pattern will be very difficult to break.

Sexual habits begin the same way. Stimulated by natural urges they become a compulsion when not tempered by loving instruction and self-control that is a conscious choice of the will until it becomes a natural response in the subconscious mind. This is far different from denial and repression.

Negative self-talk in our thoughts and subsequent speech, programs the subconscious that eventually fulfils those words in our actions and the results we see from our endeavours. The old and tested way of the saints bares much wisdom here in that we overcome compulsive unconscious sinful habits by wilfully doing the opposite virtue. By practicing the virtue in the same way, it eventually becomes an unconscious habit and a natural way of life.

In this case, we tell the truth, and keep telling the truth, no matter how many times we fail, and we do this until it becomes a habit, a habit that needs no more effort than lying did. The habit of lying began as a wilful choice in the conscious mind until it became a habit in the subconscious mind. Once embedded in the subconscious mind, a habit needs no conscious decision. Jesus said that we would know the truth and the truth would set us free. *(John 8:31-32)*

Jesus teaches that all things are possible for the one who believes, but what is this belief? Well, it is a double-edged sword. He is of course talking about believing in what God says and that will get the result that God intends, but if we do not believe, we get the result of what our unbelief dictates.

A classic account of unbelief resulting in negating God's will for our healing is in Matthew 13: 54-58. "He came to his native place and taught the people in their synagogues. They were astonished and said, 'Where did this man get such wisdom and mighty deeds? Is he not the carpenter's son? Are not his mother, named Mary and his brothers James, Joseph, Simon, and Judas? Are his sisters all with us? Where did this man get all this?' and *they took offence* at him. Jesus said to them, 'A prophet is not without honour except in his native place and in his own house.' And he did not work many mighty deeds there because of *their lack if faith*." In this case, Jesus was willing to heal them, but their unbelief prevented him from acting on their behalf.

Jesus tells us to be as though we have received. This is not so hard to understand if we consider hearing news that we have won a great deal of money. The news causes joy and excitement and we might even throw an elaborate party to celebrate even though we cannot see the money, nor is it in our possession and yet we act as though it is because we have believed the good news. The money comes into our possession a little while later and so it is with God's promises if we believe them in the same way.

Many people pray God to give them a blessing "if" it is his will. "If it be thy will" is the most common prayer and it is usually full of doubt. A person praying for peace, *if it be his will*, clearly has not believed nor knows that it is God's will that they have it, "My own peace I give you..." Jesus only used the "if" prayer once and that was in Gethsemane when asking the Father to remove the cup.

Every other time Jesus prayed, as at the tomb of Lazarus, Jesus thanked the Father for hearing his prayer and continued, "You always hear my prayer." The question for us is, can we say, "Thank you Lord, you always hear my prayer" and then act accordingly as though we already have what we asked? If not, then it is indeed, mere wishful thinking.

The Father did not remove the cup when Jesus asked so did this mean that on this occasion his Father did not answer his prayer? We know that Jesus offered only to accept whatever the Father decided was best, after which angels ministered to him.

The Father did not remove the cup as asked, but removed the need in Jesus to have the cup taken away; God met the need and in reality this is all God has ever promised; to meet our needs, and so the Father did answer Jesus' prayer, "be it done according as your will." This met the need perfectly and so Jesus was free to continue the steps of the New Covenant cut on Calvary.

For us this might mean that when asking God to supply $1000 for example, or indeed any other need, either the $1000 will come in time or the situation the money is needed for will be met and the money no longer required; the prayer is answered when the needing has stopped.

Personalising God's word has the power of making it a reality to us and that gives us hope. Ephesians 1:3, says, "Blessed be the God and Father of our Lord Jesus Christ, who has blessed us with every spiritual blessing in the heavens." This, as many promises are in the past tense and therefore we already possess them. When we personalise a statement like this it then says, "Blessed be the God and Father of my Lord Jesus Christ, he has blessed me with every spiritual blessing in the heavens. Thank you Father, I have your blessing."

In Exodus 23:25 God says that he will take all sickness from our midst. The life of Jesus and the teaching of the Apostles demonstrate the power of that promise and so we can boldly say, "Thank you Lord, you are healing my condition according as your promise." Faith as Jesus and Saint Paul teach it is the ability to believe that the impossible is possible and then act to achieve it.

Chapter 30

Measuring Saint Peter's faith

Through spoken words, we can measure another's faith and that of our own. Perhaps a good demonstration of this is to measure Jesus and Saint Peter's faith when caught in a storm on the lake in Luke 8:22-25.

One day he got into a boat with his disciples and said to them, 'Let us cross to the other side of the lake.' So they set sail, and while they were sailing he fell asleep. A storm blew over the lake, and taking in water, they were in danger. They came and woke him saying, 'Master, master, we are perishing!' He awakened, rebuked the wind and the waves, and they subsided and there was a calm. Then he asked them, "Where is your faith?" That is a good question and Jesus does not elaborate on this and neither do they answer, they are awestruck and talked amongst themselves.

As we wonder why Jesus did not press them for an answer, we might want to consider that it was to impress upon their minds the situation and their response in contrast to Jesus' response. The more they talked and the more they thought about it, the whole event would have pierced their conscious thought that by its nature begged an answer; it kept them aware and alert to what Jesus was saying and doing.

We can also see by his question that faith was the real issue and that he expected them to have enough not to fear the circumstances. The faith that Jesus expected them to have would have been sufficient to overcome the storm without having to disturb his sleep. To grasp this let us take a systematic look at the scenario and the words used in it.

Although not named, we can accept that all twelve disciples were present including Peter and others that were professional fishers - Peter was an experienced boatman who had sailed that lake many times in his life and we can reasonably assume he did this in all weathers, even storms. It was not the same for Matthew the tax collector and some of the others and we might expect them to be apprehensive in a dangerous situation. In this light, we could equally expect that Peter and the other experienced men might comfort and encourage the others and take control of the situation but he did not. On the contrary, Peter panicked and received a rebuke along with the rest.

To get a clearer picture of the faith-lesson Jesus is demonstrating let us imagine a conversation between Jesus and Peter after asking, "Where is your faith?" This will help us to measure Peter's faith and so, perhaps the conversation would have gone something like this. "Peter, were you afraid when I asked to go to the other side of the lake? No Lord I was not afraid. Peter, were you afraid when I fell asleep? No Lord, I was not afraid. Peter, were you afraid when we were out on the lake? No Lord I was not afraid to be out on the lake. Peter, were you afraid when you saw the dark clouds rolling in? No Lord I was not afraid. Peter, were you afraid when the wind and rain became strong? No Lord, I was not afraid, but I was getting a little worried. Peter, when the storm became strong and the waves were filling the boat, were you afraid? Yes Lord, I was afraid. Peter, when you were afraid, did you think you would die? Yes Lord, I was afraid that I would die."

In this interplay, we can see Peter's measure of faith from no fear at all to absolute panic in fear of death in the way he answered Jesus. We can learn then, that the opposite of faith is fear, and all fear linked to death.

What then, can we learn about Jesus? He was asleep in the midst of the storm, and he would have remained so if they had not awoken him. Could this be because he was so tired that even the worst storm could not disturb him? On the other hand, could it be that he did not care about his disciple's lives or his own? Reason dictates that both these are wrong, so, why did Jesus continue to sleep regardless of the circumstances?

To understand this we need to go back to what Jesus said when he got into the boat and then what he did after speaking. Jesus said, "Let us cross to the other side of the lake." Then he went to sleep. Jesus had spoken his faith about reaching the other side. This faith did not entertain the idea that anything would stop the outcome of what he said and so he could rest and sleep in peace knowing all will be well. We could say that Jesus had faith in his own words and believed what he said would happen, would in fact happen regardless of the circumstances.

This was not the case for the disciples who forgot what Jesus had said when the circumstances changed for the worst. Had they believed and had faith in what Jesus had said, they would not have panicked and would not have feared death as the result. It is the same in our lives when we take our attention from what Jesus has said and let the circumstances overwhelm us. When we do this, we too think that Jesus is fast asleep and does not care about the predicaments in which often we find ourselves. Jesus has spoken, and that is enough to get the job done. The disciples focused on the problem and lost sight of the solution and this resulted in a fear of dying. There was no need for this because Jesus is the Lord of the circumstance.

In our case, we cannot put our faith in what we do not know. If we do not know what Jesus has to say, then we cannot put our faith in it. This means that we must of necessity, know the Word of God because faith comes by hearing, and hearing by the Word of God. *(Romans 10:17)*

Without knowledge of God's Word, we will remain ignorant in our circumstances and be in danger of building a faith on presumption and supposition rather than a faith built on the solid rock of God's promises. Our assumptions will have no more effect on the circumstances we find ourselves in than did the disciples ability to still the storm on the lake. In this case, we could also sin by anger that God does not care about us, and the more this prevails, the more we will doubt until faith is gone and we live in poverty, and at worst, fear will destroy us.

Another case worth investigation is Peter's experience of walking on the water recorded in Matthew 14:22-33. On this occasion the disciples has set out to the other side of the Sea of Galilee without Jesus who remained to dismiss the crowds and went to the mountain to pray. He remained there until evening and the disciples, several kilometres from shore, are in a storm, tossed by the waves. In the fourth watch of the night, the disciples saw Jesus walking on the water towards them and thinking it was a ghost, they were terrified.

Jesus spoke and said to them, "Take courage, it is I; do not be afraid." Peter called to him and said, "Lord, if it is you, command me to come to you on the water." Jesus said, "Come." Peter got out of the boat and began to walk on the water towards Jesus, but when he saw the ferocity of the wind and the storm, he became *afraid*, began to sink and cried, "Lord, save me." Immediately Jesus stretched out his hand and caught him, and said to him, "O you of little faith, why did you doubt?"

Again, there are several lessons for us in this scenario and perhaps the first is that Jesus was in prayer before walking across the water. Although there is no record of what Jesus was praying about, it is clear that the boat had already left when he dismissed the crowds. Whatever he prayed or why is not so much the point as the fact that he was in prayer before such a miraculous feat and we note that Jesus would do this often as at the tomb of Lazarus before raising him from death.

The first thing we can learn before we embark on some bold venture or step out to minister is that prayer should precede it so that we are in the will of God and under his anointing for the task.

The circumstances were tumultuous when Jesus approached and although Jesus announced himself by encouraging them, Peter did not just jump out of the boat without first checking if it was indeed Jesus on the water. Albeit from fear of a ghost, he had never the less wisely put the spirit to the test as Saint John later taught, by asking Jesus to call him. *(1John 4:1-3)*

The double lesson here is that we should not just trust every spirit that seems to be of Jesus and certainly not to act until confirmed that it is; Peter did not act until he knew that God wanted him to. This teaches us that we should not presume to minister unless we are called to do so and it is confirmed by a competent authority.

In the lesson of faith, we note that when Peter took his eyes off Jesus and from what he had spoken to him, the circumstances overwhelmed him and he began to sink. It can be the same for us when we let the situations replace Jesus as the Lord of the circumstance; when sickness prevails, it can become easier to focus on the symptoms than on the answer. Focussing his attention on the circumstance surrounding him, Peter's faith turned to fear and he sank.

184

This can be the same for us; we sink into despair as we see the situation as hopeless.

With prostate cancer advancing despite asking God for healing, and at the same time writing my book 12 Steps to Divine Healing, I could have been distracted in my faith in God's promises and focussed on the fear of not recovering.

During that time, I was tempted many times to give up or compromise the book but I did not. In this case, with the storm of cancer's symptoms raging worse as time went on, it was easy to give up. Instead, I kept my eyes on Jesus and his promises, and two years later immediately after publishing the book, eight biopsies showed no sign of cancer. The professor of urology declared me cancer free and I remain so today.

Saint Paul in Ephesians 6:13-14 exhorts us to hold our ground and stand fast *(in faith)* when circumstances prevail against us. Although Peter wavered and began to sink, we can take courage from two things; the first is that Jesus immediately helped Peter when his faith dwindled and in spite of his measure of faith only lasting a short while, Peter did walk on the water when he obeyed God's Word and kept his eyes on Jesus.

Unless tempered by faith and grace, human nature like water, will always take the least line of resistance, flow downhill and avoid obstacles, whereas grace will measure up to the task and faith will remove the mountain. In the case of personal problems, we can easily avoid conflict or shove the problem under the carpet. Of course, this does not remove the obstacles and when enough rubbish is under the carpet, it will eventually show an ugly lump usually to our great embarrassment when asked what it is. As someone once said, "Denial is not a river in Egypt."

When faced with resolving difficult problems with people, instead of running from our Goliaths, we will have more success by taking a few seconds of care in the first place and that will save a lifetime of regret.

Unless we know God's Word, we will not know his will. If we do not know his will, we cannot do his will on earth as Jesus taught in the Lord's Prayer. Those thinking it not possible to know his will, need to read John's Gospel carefully underlining every mention of the word, *word*. I have called this the Gospel of the Word because it begins, as did this book with the genesis of the Logos and the Rhema. John 17:3, says, "Now this is eternal life, that they should know you, the only true God, and the one whom you sent, Jesus Christ."

We can know God; in fact, it is his will that we know him because that knowledge gives us eternal life by faith in his Word, Jesus, the Word made flesh and what Jesus says reveals God's will. Without this knowledge, we are lost in the storm, and like the disciples, that will be the measure of our faith. On the other hand, if we put our faith in God's Word and do what he says, our faith will grow so strong that no storm will overcome us anymore than it did Jesus.

Chapter 31

Faith sees. Faith speaks.
Faith acts. Faith gets results

The three basic actions of faith: seeing, speaking and acting are the preceding factors to achieving a result. One of the best examples is in Acts 3:1-10 that records the healing of the crippled beggar at the Beautiful Gate by Peter and John. To see these actions we will read the text and then look at the event unfolding. This will make more sense of the term, 'We walk by faith, not by sight.'

"Now Peter and John were going up to the temple for the three o'clock hour of prayer. And a man crippled from birth was carried and placed at the gate of the temple called 'the Beautiful Gate' every day to beg for alms from the people who entered the temple. When he saw Peter and John about to go into the temple, he asked for alms. But Peter looked intently at him, as did John, and said, 'Look at us.' He paid attention to them, expecting to receive something from them. Peter said, 'I have neither silver nor gold, but what I do have I give to you: in the name of Jesus the Nazorean, rise and walk.' Then Peter took him by the right hand and raised him up, and immediately his feet and ankles grew strong. He leaped up, stood, and walked around and went into the temple with them, walking and jumping and praising God."

Firstly, since Peter and John went to worship each day at the three o'clock service, this was not the first time they had seen this crippled beggar, nor was it the first time that he had seen them. The question arises as to why this man did not receive his health on a previous occasion. This seems to be a question of faith and anointing both of which need to be present to bring a result. On this occasion, both endowments were present and so Peter gained the man's attention and spoke out his faith, "In the name of Jesus the Nazorean, rise and walk,"

Peter does not pray but commands the man in Jesus' Name; he speaks to the mountain as Jesus had previously taught him to do. Hearing these words of faith from Peter the man does not immediately jump to his feet. In fact, he remains crippled. Peter has seen and spoken but there is no result. If at this point, Peter had relied on what he could see in the natural he would have given up and left the man crippled.

It is here that many Christians give up when not seeing an immediate result. Peter now acts and takes the man by the hand pulling him up even though his legs are still crippled. It is not until Peter has pulled the man to his feet that the healing takes place and the man stands on his own strength for the first time in his life. In this miracle, we see the three laws of faith; seeing, speaking, acting, and these procure the result.

Luke 5:17-26 and Mark 2:12 demonstrate this in Jesus' ministry. On this occasion, we see that the anointing to heal could be noticed, "And the power of the Lord was with him for healing." For Luke and Mark to make note of this, tells us that the anointing to heal is evident when it is present, although not activated until the need arises; faith is resident. As the men bring their paralytic friend to Jesus, verse 20 says, "When he saw their faith." Clearly, faith is visible. If it were not, Jesus would not see it in them and Luke would not comment on it. Because he saw their faith

188

demonstrated by their effort to get their friend to him, Jesus acted and we read how the man was completely set free from his infirmity.

In this scene, there are several key factors at work. The first is that the anointing is present in Jesus beforehand. In the case of Peter and John, we also see that they were on the way to the temple for the hour of prayer. Under the anointing, Jesus can see that faith is present in the men. Because a large crowd is present seeking something from Jesus, we can reasonably accept that there was something different about these men and their crippled friend. The obvious reason is that they broke through the roof to get their friend to Jesus. Their determination, love and persistence showed their faith in what they were doing but there seems to be more to it than this.

In our own experience, we might see people clamour to get in a healing line for prayer only to receive little or no result after ministry. Healing in the name of Jesus is not a magic incantation; it requires faith in the name, that is, the person, and this is required of both the minister and the person seeking prayer.

In order to get the people's faith to level where they can believe for a result, the preceding acts of worship and the message from the Word of God is very important. During a time of healing ministry, people will line up for prayer; the healing teams will go to people and pray for them. Very often, this can take a considerable amount of time and many leave in the same condition in which they came.

It remains a mystery as to why some receive healing and some do not, but there are some important things to consider that will greatly reduce our apparent failure. The first consideration is the anointing. As we have seen, Mark and Luke noted that the anointing to heal was present with

Jesus beforehand. People operating publicly in a recognised healing ministry must accept by faith that they have the anointing for this ministry because they will not always "feel" anointed. Having great compassion or a great desire to see people healed is not enough; only the anointing is sufficient for this.

Another consideration is whether the people seeking prayer are themselves in or under the anointing. If they are not, then it will take a long time praying for them, we might not see a good result and this will not build faith in those that observe it. If the anointing is present in the person seeking prayer, there will be no need for prayers of many words or counselling while ministering, very often the person will receive without even touching them or saying anything.

In order to achieve this it is necessary for the ministers to discern where the anointing is present upon a person and go to those people first. This is the gift of discerning of spirits; a seeing gift that can look into the spirit realm seeing exactly what spirit is in operation at any given time. *(1Corintians 12:10)* Apart from the human spirit, an evil spirit, or an angel, we are seeking the Holy Spirit in action upon the person.

Spoken in faith, the person recognises the anointing on the words or the touch and it triggers their faith to receive what they believe. If the healing ministries go to those in the anointing first, there will be a quicker result, and seeing this, it will build the faith of those who observe it; when that faith is present, there is more chance of a result.

Jesus speaks the words of faith and because the people believed what they heard, *(Romans 10:17)* they received the resulting health. It is worth noting that in these cases Jesus does not pray for healing, he declares the result by faith as he had demonstrated in Matthew 21:18-22 and

Matthew 24:32-35. The hearer, believing what he said acts on it, this act of faith in union with Jesus brings the desired result, and this is what happened with the paralysed man.

Perhaps the reasons for many people emphasising spiritual rather than physical healing are clear in this situation. The first thing that Jesus said regarding their faith was, "Your sins are forgiven." This brings a verbal retort from the Pharisees present, and Jesus knowing the murmuring of their hearts, asks if it easier to say to the man that he has forgiveness or to tell him to rise, take up his bed and walk? "To prove that the son of man has the power to forgive sins, I say to you, rise, take up your bed, and go home." The man did. However, it was not until the man acted on what Jesus said that he experienced the result. This raises the question regarding which is easier, forgiveness, or physical healing.

Clearly, forgiveness is easier simply because we cannot check that out as we can check the physical result. Fearing failure, many Christians stop at the forgiveness and spiritual healing. In this case, Jesus used the physical manifestation to prove the spiritual reality of restoration contained in the jubilee promises.

Another example of the ministry of the Word during an act of worship is clear in the account of the woman crippled by a spirit and related to the spiritual source. "He was teaching in a synagogue on the Sabbath and a woman was there who for eighteen years had been crippled by a spirit; she was bent over, completely incapable of standing erect. When Jesus saw her, he called to her and said, 'Woman, you are free from your infirmity.' He laid hands on her, and at once she stood up straight and glorified God." *(Luke 13:10-13)*

The woman is present during a worship service; Jesus is the preacher and evangelist giving the teaching.

191

While he is teaching, we see the charismatic gift of the word of knowledge come into operation. *(1Corinthians 12:8)* The charismatic gifts of the Holy Spirit reveal to Jesus that the Father desires to heal the woman who has a covenant with him through Abraham. It also reveals the true nature of the problem through the gift of the discerning of spirits. Jesus sees what spirit is responsible for her infirmity and Jesus speaks the Father's will for the woman.

Again, it is important to understand that Jesus did not pray for this woman; he declared her healing, and only then did he place his hands on her; Jesus acted on the faith he declared. The woman had heard Jesus teaching in the service and when he spoke, directly to her, she believed what she heard and the touch confirmed it. Her faith thus triggered, she acted and stood up and the blessings that belonged to her by divine right enshrined in the covenant of Abraham came into effect.

In the case of the woman with the issue of blood in Luke 8:40-46, we see a different operation of faith in that the woman's faith when touching the hem of Jesus' garment releases power from Jesus even though he did not know she was present to him. Jesus recognised what happened even in the midst of others who are also touching him. The difference is that this woman touched him with faith and it was her faith that connected with the anointing on Jesus to release the power to heal and Jesus felt it; faith releases the anointing.

It is certain that this woman did not just happen upon Jesus. She had heard about him, believed what she heard and acted on it. She spoke faith when she said to herself that she only needed to touch the hem of his garment to be healed and even though she was unclean and should not have been there let alone touch Jesus or anyone else her faith justified her action.

This would be the same situation with Peter and John. In some translations of the Bible, it says that Peter and John saw the cripple's faith and then looked intently at him. Looking intently is the action of the anointing that is present at that time.

As in Jesus' case, it discerns that faith is present. Seeing the cripple's faith as they look intently at him, Peter speaks. At this point, it is easy for us to jump immediately to the result and miss the operation of faith and the action that gives the result.

As we have noted previously, only after gaining the man's attention does Peter speak in the name of Jesus Christ the Nazorean but the man does not immediately jump to his feet. In fact, at this point the man remains a cripple. If we were to speak out our faith in the name of Jesus and the situation remained unchanged, we might give up, thinking that faith or the name of Jesus did not work. As we look closer at Peter's situation, we can see that when he saw faith present, he spoke specifically his faith, clearly identified in whose name he spoke, and then acted upon it. Only when Peter pulled the man to his feet were his ankles strong and he then stood up. Peter acted on faith and then we see the result.

Peter's faith was in the person of Jesus, and using his power of attorney spoke and acted. In this situation, as with those previously mentioned, the three principles of faith are present: seeing, speaking, acting and then, the result.

This man, crippled at birth, sat at the temple every day and everyone in the temple knew this. When they saw the man leaping and praising God, it activated their faith and many came to believe that Jesus is Lord. In this way, the signs and wonders testify that the words spoken can be believed and this is why healing is very much part of the

193

evangelisation process. This brings conversion to those that have no faith at the beginning; the result is salvation, the ultimate spiritual healing.

Chapter 32

Faith healed HIV/AIDS and overcame death

David had a good upbringing in a small country town in Western Australia. His Christian life began in the Anglican Church where the Bible played a strong role from an early age. As much as he loved reading it, he did not see reflected in the people around him the healings and miracles of which the Bible spoke. As he grew into teenage years he stopped attending church and began a homosexual lifestyle after experiencing a sexual seduction by an older male at a youth camp.

In his early twenties, David met a young Catholic and they became very good friends. One day, David found a book belonging to his friend that spoke about God's healing and charismatic gifts. At this discovery, he asked his friend to explain it to him, which his friend gladly did. The result was that David accepted Jesus as his Lord and made a vow of celibacy as the only option for someone with a same sex attraction.

Later, after reading an advertisement for a Flame Ministries International Set My People on Fire seminar, David knew somehow that this is where he was to be, and along with his friend registered for the fifteen-week course. During the weeks, David's faith and belief in Christ grew stronger and a burning desire to serve the Gospel gripped his heart. Some months after completing the seminar, David

195

and his friend joined Flame Ministries International and on May 3 1994, he became a Catholic.

The day after his Confirmation, he left Australia and assisted me on a mission in England to present Set My People on Fire in Birmingham and Peterborough. Both young men taught sessions in the seminars, but the nine months spent in often-difficult circumstances in a foreign country took its toll. Towards the end of the mission, David and his best friend experienced a very painful split and their long close friendship ended.

After returning to Australia, they gave up ministry and the Church, rejected Jesus, and for the next seven years lived a very hedonistic homosexual drug lifestyle. This culminated with David binge drinking, becoming a workaholic resulting in clinical depression and drug addiction, using crystal-meth, cocaine, ecstasy, marijuana and speed, gay prostitution, having suicidal tendencies and contracting AIDS with little hope of survival.

Eventually David's downhill spiral cost him his job, his drug debts also put his life in danger, and he declared bankruptcy loosing everything that he had including his well-paid and prominent job as a bank officer. Having nowhere to go, David went home to his mother but kept his addiction a secret. "That was until one night when I didn't have my comedown supplies with me and I hit the bottom in a bad way and knew it couldn't be a secret anymore."

That night whilst in a pit of despair, he saw something in the corner of his eye. Startled, he immediately turned around to see Jesus standing there. "I said Oh, it's you. He was just smiling, looking into my heart and I knew it was Jesus and knew that everything would be OK."

After this, David decided to leave that life behind and attended our St. Mary's Cathedral Praise Meeting in Perth where, after a seven-year absence, I welcomed David

196

and his friend without question with tears of joy and open arms. Later, they both made their confessions and turned back to Christ. There were no withdrawal symptoms from the addictive drugs and they recommitted themselves to serve the Church through Flame Ministries International once more.

A year later, immediately after the Flame Ministries 2003 Congress, David became ill with severe pneumonia. The diagnosis at Royal Perth Hospital showed full-blown HIV/AIDS: David had no immune system.

I visited David in hospital and prayed with him. I also encouraged him to use the time to get closer to Jesus, who is the Way, the Truth, and the Life, and to meditate on the truth that God really does love him and to resist the power of the threat of death; God created the immune system and so we agreed that God could restore it. David reasoned by faith that there was no point to God saving him from a life of drug addiction and homosexuality to serve him once more in the work of evangelisation only to let him die of HIV/AIDS.

David believed and put his faith in God's love for him and although rushed to hospital close to death on several occasions, he maintained his faith in God's promises; the reliable promises of God on which faith is the foundation. All the FMI members constantly supported David in prayer.

On one occasion, after hearing that David was in hospital in a critical state, I stopped the Set My People on Fire Seminar, and over the mobile phone, the delegates and all present sang David's favourite praise song and prayed for his healing. David did not give up hope and his faith grew in the power of the Word of God that Jesus could fully restore his immune system even though he was close to death several times.

197

David's faith was rewarded and a year later at our 2004 Congress, Receiving the Mercy of God, he shared his amazing testimony showing the letter from the hospital that declared him HIV/AIDS free. David showed the graph of his restored immune system on a T-Cell Recovery Chart. The chart showed a line from no T-Cells to a restored immune system.

David read out the letter from the specialist written one month after beginning treatment; the specialist wrote, "David returned to Immunology Clinic today for the one-month review after his commencement of HIV+ medication. He has had the most remarkable increase in CD4 count I have ever seen in one month's time. His CD4 count has gone from 68 (4%) up to 384 (12%) in only four week's time."

While there were still signs of HIV, David no longer had AIDS. Just six months later blood tests confirmed that there was no HIV. To satisfy his mind David visited his doctor for a second opinion. David said, "The doctor read the reports, sat back in his chair, paused for a while and excitedly exclaimed, 'These results are truly miraculous'."

David is now well and in love with Denise who is a member of the Flame Music Ministry and they have begun a committed relationship. God is using him in the ministry of preaching the Gospel once more. Since then his testimony alone has had dramatic effects on other young people and most especially those struggling with AIDS, drug addictions and homosexuality of all ages, and serves to demonstrate that life without faith in Jesus is as good as being dead. So far, David has shared his testimony in Australia, Uganda, Portugal, United Kingdom, USA and Indonesia where his message has given hope to those that suffer.

David's faith, challenged in the fires of a death penalty from HIV/AIDS was tested *(dokimion)* but he did not let go of Jesus or his faith in Jesus' promises no matter what seemed in the natural to be taking place. David's faith in the midst of a worsening crisis justified him and he is now healthy. David viewed himself as a new creation in Christ. In this, he viewed himself as healed, and the only death present to him was that to the old life and its consequences; he was born anew and by God's divine decree had a right to his life, and that life more abundantly.

The Greek word for Life is zoë in John 10:10. Not just related to our earthly time span, zoë means to have life as a principle, life in the absolute sense, life as God has in himself as God and that which he gave Jesus to have in himself as the Son of God which Jesus manifest in the world and gave to have in us. The word *abundantly* means a fullness; sufficiency; wealth; copiousness; profusion and great to overflowing. This why Jesus came and this is what God gave David to have in himself.

Chapter 33

Charismatic Faith and raising the dead

Raising the dead covered in my book 12 Steps to Divine Healing is worth repeating because the act of faith and the various charismatic gifts are imperative in this. Jesus used these gifts and Saint Paul teaches extensively on them. In addition, they are common supernatural manifestations in the lives of the men and women throughout Holy Scripture. Only after Pentecost did the Holy Spirit dwell in man as a permanent guest and therefore manifests these gifts according as he wills in those open to his anointing on an ongoing basis by faith.

The primary gift of the Holy Spirit in raising the dead is the charismatic gift of *(special)* faith, and as we have noted, this is different from the virtue of faith that enables us to believe in the principles set forth in the Bible or Church teaching. Because Saint Paul says, "To another, faith" we can become confused about how faith operates in the life of a believer. This misunderstanding is a likely cause for people blaming another person's lack of faith if they do not see a result when praying for them, especially for healing.

The charismatic gift of faith is instant, absolute, and peaceful and has no doubts. It speaks precisely and moves mountains. Although resident by virtue of the Holy Spirit within us, unlike the virtue of faith it is only manifest when needed as in the case of Peter and John with the cripple at the Beautiful Gate. When it is manifest, it takes the virtue of faith built on the Word of God to speak and act on what the Holy Spirit prompts. This is so when someone moved to speak to a dead body in order that it might live, causes life to flow into dead flesh.

This was the case when a Catholic nun collapsed from a heart attack at our praise meeting on Thursday 15 October 1992. The situation was a night of powerful praise and deep worship. The presence of God was evident and the anointing very strong. We had moved into the realm of the miraculous but nothing of consequence happened until after the meeting had closed.

Whilst the people were having refreshments and I was still in the auditorium engaged in a conversation, a man came and said that Sister had collapsed in the kitchen and appeared to have died from a massive heart attack.

Ordinarily, news like this could throw you, but for some reason I was perfectly calm and untroubled and told him not to worry because she would be all right and the conversation with the troubled woman continued.

Leaving the auditorium a short while later and entering the kitchen, I saw Sister collapsed on the floor with people standing around weeping and trying not to panic. Again, strangely calm, untroubled and certain of the outcome, the people were encouraged not to worry and assured that she would be all right.

Kneeling to check on Sister, I saw that her normal ruddy complexion and features were not recognisable. Before this, an ex-nurse had checked for vital signs but found none. I sent one of the men to get an ambulance and he ran to the Royal Perth Hospital a short distance away. Checking her pulse and breath, neither was functional and her skin was stone cold, yellow-grey and clammy with no substance. Her eyes were open, starring unblinking at the ceiling. They were colourless, flat and had no moisture whatsoever and so it seemed clear to me from all the signs present that she had died.

Holding her hand and looking into her flat dry colourless eyes, I spoke *(Rhema)* calmly, quietly, and firmly to her. "Sister, in the name of Jesus - come back. Come on Sister, you can do it. Stand up. I command you in the name of Jesus to stand up."

I continued this way for ten to fifteen minutes when suddenly she blinked, took a deep breath and her eyes swelled to their normal shape as the colour and moisture returned. At the same time, a flush of healthy pink flowed from her grey hairline all through her face and body, and as it reached her hands, the heat and firmness of life returned. At that moment, she breathed out, "Aaah... What happened?"

A few moments later, she stood up and drank a cup of tea handed to her by one of the women. At this time, the paramedics came and asked where the body was. I introduced them to Sister and they asked what had happened. After a short explanation, they took her to the hospital shaking their heads in a state of bewilderment as Sister laughed and joked with them all the way.

The following week Sister told about the barrage of tests from her doctors. She had been suffering for a long time and was due for a triple bypass operation. After thorough examinations, her cardiologists could find nothing wrong with her heart. "They told me that my heart was as strong as a horse," she said with a beaming Irish smile.

Later we informed the Archbishop and relevant priests. The Archbishop accepted the report and referred to it in a letter as "a remarkable recovery."

Sister did not need an operation, God had healed the heart condition and Sister could now enjoy her health and a long life. It was over half an hour from when Sister collapsed to when she recovered and we know that after a few minutes, a person's brain cells begin to die and they suffer brain damage that remains after recovery. In this case, there was no brain damage at all. On the contrary, Sister was alert and bright when she recovered.

In this remarkable event, some very important points sum up what we have said so far regarding faith, worship, and anointing. The first is the heartfelt praise during the meeting. Praise is the language of faith, especially praise using the gift of tongues, and the Bible tells us that God dwells in the praise of his people.

As on the day of Pentecost, the anointing of the Holy Spirit is present in power when God's people yield in humility to heartfelt praise and worship. This presence of the Holy Spirit manifests the charismatic gifts in those open to his action. The Holy Spirit reveals the mind of God and through the word gifts, the people know God's purposes and it builds up their faith. In this case, it was the realisation that we had entered the realm of the miraculous.

When this tragedy occurred, no one presumed to minister, but rightly called the leader to deal with it. Order and obedience was conducive to what happened next. Through the charismatic gift of (special) faith, doubt is not present in the (Rhema) words spoken and it brought forth the gift of the working of miracles that caused a dead body to respond with life. Finally, the gifts of healing cured the heart and restored it to perfect health. All this gave glory to God, as did the accounts we read in the Bible. The charismatic gifts involved with raising the dead are, faith, miracles and healing.

Before this event, I did not know that my faith was sufficient to raise the dead. However, by spending quality time in the Word of God and in prayer, my faith had grown to such a degree over the years that when needed it came into force without another thought. In this whole event, I did not pray for God to raise Sister. Like Jesus in the synagogue and Peter and John at the Beautiful Gate, I spoke the (Rhema) words of faith as the Holy Spirit prompted and faith worked the miracle when activated.

Most interesting is the fact that a dead body is incapable of having faith; it cannot hear in order to respond. This means that the one operating in faith does not always need to rely on another's faith to be effective; this is comforting when we are praying for the sick or troubled.

As we have discovered in chapter 31, it remains important to create an atmosphere of faith for them. This is because their malady often robs their faith and so the one ministering relies on the anointing of the Holy Spirit and acts in faith on their behalf.

When this happens in a faith-filled environment, it has amazing results. Then again, just as Jesus could not heal people in Nazareth due to their lack of faith, so it is with those we pray for when they come to us. It is paramount therefore that we create a faith-filled environment in order for them to receive and the signs and wonders are what follow the preaching of the Word of God. This is why meetings or services of this nature flow from worship, preaching, and then ministry.

Two more accounts of healing and raising the dead through speaking out the words of faith are in Acts 9:32-43. Aeneas had been confined to bed for eight years due to paralysis. When Peter arrived at Lydda, he visited Aeneas. Peter said to him, "Aeneas, Jesus Christ heals you. Get up and make your bed." Aeneas got up immediately and made his bed. Later, Peter went to Joppa to see a disciple by the name of Tabitha who had died. When he enters the room, he removes the mourners, kneels down, and prays. Then he turns to her body and says, "Tabitha, rise up." He then gave her his hand and raised her up.

In this case, the first thing that Peter did was to remove all negativity and doubt by dismissing the mourners and Jesus did the same thing in his ministry. The next thing that Peter did was to pray. Of course, we do not know what he prayed or for how long, nor do we know how Peter prayed but we can get an idea about this because Jesus did the same thing at the tomb of Lazarus before calling him forth.

We can know therefore that it is important to be in the will God and under his anointing before we minister and this is likely what Peter did too. In this case, the praise meeting was the prayer that brought the anointing. Peter did not pray over Tabitha, he spoke *(Rhema)* directly to the dead body and it responded exactly as he had spoken. This was the same when Jesus commanded Lazarus and it was the same when I commanded Sister to stand up and come back.

In the case of Sister, a woman throwing a tantrum and drawing attention because she could not have her own way left the auditorium and the people present were then encouraged so that they would not doubt.

Not known for his short homilies, Saint Paul was very considerate. On one occasion, he begins preaching around six in the evening and is still talking at midnight when a young man named Eutychus sitting on the window ledge nods off *(as some parishioners are still prone to do)* and plummets two stories to his death! Paul stops talking, calmly walks down to the street, goes to the body, lies on top of it and breaths into the boy who promptly comes back to life no worse off for the experience. Saint Paul calmly goes back upstairs and continues his homily until dawn. *(Acts 20:7-12)*

205

It is certain that those early Christians, seeing by faith what could not be seen in the future would have rejoiced at someone else taking the time to explain Hebrews 11:1 instead of Saint Paul because at least they got home in time for an early breakfast and maybe a 'cuppa' after Mass.

It is wonderful to see how similar each of these accounts are, most especially in our day and age when most of us do not expect the same things to happen in our lives as they did in the Bible. It should not surprise us if they do and there is no mystery; Jesus is the same yesterday, today and tomorrow; God has not changed the way he operates because God does not change and so what we read in the Word of God is supremely reliable. Setting our faith on God's Word rather than the circumstances always affects the circumstance in which we find ourselves for our good and the good of others.

It must be kept in mind that these are not techniques used, otherwise we will make the same error as Simon the magician in Acts 8:9-25 and experience the same failure and receive the same reproach. All of these accounts are by way of obedience to God's will in humble submission and acting in faith; faith is the ability to believe that the impossible is possible, and then to go about achieving it and as we have now discovered, faith plus works equals results.

In both the cases of David and Sister, faith spoken and then acted upon beats the power of death and the result is always life and life more abundantly and this is the substance of our hope. *(John 10:10)*

Chapter 34

Words and the Law of Faith

As we have seen so far, speaking the word of faith is paramount to success just as speaking the words of doubt result in failure, or in reality, success in what we do not want to happen or achieve. Jesus does not ask us to pray the mountain to move but to speak to the mountain without doubt and it will move. From the very beginning of Genesis, God speaks and creation and the entire universe come into being.

John's Gospel reflects that when he explains that Jesus is the Word from the beginning. In Jesus, God spoke with a human voice telling us to speak to the mountain, speak to the mulberry tree, and to act on his words. He tells us that if we remain in his word and his words remain in us, we will bear much fruit: a fruit that will last, eternally. Saint Paul tells us that faith comes by hearing the Word of God.

The Gospel is an open proclamation and not just something believed in an internal personal way. Even our human words have a negative or positive effect and Jesus warns about idle words that fall from our lips and tells us that we are accountable for every unguarded word. He tells us that by our words, acquittal or condemnation is the result. Throughout the Bible, the idea of words is a constant thread in God's revelation of faith. The words we speak reveal our inner belief. This is why we need a renewal in the spirit of our minds through the Word of God. We must put on the mind of Christ because as we think, so we speak.

The fundamental rule of faith is that the only reality that God recognises is his Word. He does not change his word to suit the circumstances, but changes circumstances to suit his word, and this includes the entire universe; "God's word is irresistible, destroys all other realities, and creates new ones." *(Ken Chant)*

When God speaks, his word becomes law. He does not use words for the sake of it - when he speaks it is an eternal reality that cannot be broken or retracted unless God speaks again revealing something else. Satan, whose original name was Lucifer and the ministering cherub to the Word at the Throne, knows this. Because he is not omnipotent or omnipresent or has any godly characteristics at all, he seeks to cause God to speak in order to bring a new reality and we see this unfold in the book of Job.

Because God has spoken on behalf of Job, it is an irrevocable law in his regard as God extols his virtues. Satan wants to destroy Job but cannot because he is in God's favour and under his protection. In order to get God to speak, Satan challenges God regarding Job's fidelity to him. God responds saying that he believes in Job but Satan can take his belongings but not to touch Job and Satan duly goes about doing just that, legally.

Not satisfied with destroying everything that is precious to Job he returns to God who again affirms Job's loyalty and fidelity. Satan however offers another challenge to prove his accusations that Job will reject God and so God gives Satan permission to take Job but to leave his soul intact. Satan then causes Job to burst out in boils. In the chapters following from three onwards we read Job's speech that begins with cursing the day he was born. For another thirty-four chapters we read the speeches of Job and his friends debating the reason and cause of Job's suffering because in their minds Job had sinned. Finally, in chapter thirty-eight God speaks and challenges Job even to the origin of the universe. Job finally repents and God restores him because what God has said to Job becomes a new law that overrides the words that he spoke to Satan regarding Job.

God then turns to Job's friends and says to Eliphaz, "I am angry with you and with your two friends; for you have not *spoken* rightly concerning me, as has my servant Job." God delivers them to Job and tells them that he will accept whatever Job *says* on their behalf because he will *listen* to Job's *prayers* and not theirs. The end of the book shows Job restored seven times greater and living another 140 years in order to enjoy the family and honour that he had lost.

In this interplay, we are seeing Satan engaging God in order to get him to speak. God has already spoken regarding Job saying that he is faithful and loves God more than anyone on earth. He is under God's protection and God's spoken blessings regarding his life. Satan knows that God's word is law once spoken and to cause God to take a different view of Job will give Satan the authority to act on God's word in order to destroy him. We do note however, that Satan can do no more than God allows and in the end of his trial Job is restored seven times greater than before because God's spoken word in Job's favour creates a new reality.

Abraham, the man of faith, also knew the law of words. When God comes down to destroy Sodom and Gomorrah he tells Abraham his purpose and this purpose is the reality. In typical semitic bargaining mode, Abraham knows that what God has said is his law and so he speaks to God asking if God would destroy the cities if he found 50 good men. The question requires an answer and Abraham knows that whatever God says becomes law and creates a new reality. The risk is that God might reiterate his original purpose and no more conversation would ensue. God responds and says that he will not destroy the cities if there are 50 good men and now this condition is a new law and a new reality. Abraham knows that it is doubtful that 50 are there and so he speaks again asking if God would destroy the cities for 45 good men and God agrees for 45.

Abraham continues giving God reasons to agree with him and with each response from God a new law is in place and so Abraham continues to bargain God down to 10 good men. At this last agreement, God departs for Sodom and Gomorrah, and because not even ten good men were there, the cities reap destruction.

It is interesting to note that if God had found ten good men, then all those that lived there, even in their depravity, would have lived. At each bargaining encounter, God's response becomes his law and as he speaks it to Abraham, he creates a new reality. *(Genesis 18:16-33)*

In the case of the Roman centurion's servant, we see the same situation. The centurion says to Jesus that he only needs to *speak* the word and his servant will recover and gives examples of how the laws of Caesar work for him giving him authority to command others; to hear the centurion is to hear Caesar because it is Caesar's law and thus the only reality that Caesar and the empire recognises.

The Centurion however recognises that Jesus is operating under a higher authority and whatever he says will happen. Jesus impressed by this faith grants his request. When Jesus says, "As you have believed, let it be done for you" the law of God's spoken word is enacted and because the only reality that God recognises is his Word it destroys the reality of the servant's sickness and creates an new reality of health and the servant recovers. *(Matthew 8:5-13)*

In the case of the Canaanite woman's faith, we see this again. The woman has no covenant rights anymore than the Roman centurion did, and when she asks Jesus to deliver her daughter from a demon, unlike his response to the centurion, Jesus does not reply.

The disciples ask Jesus to send her away because she is a nuisance. Jesus tells them that he is there for the lost sheep of Israel and refuses her request, but the woman continues to plead with him asking Jesus to help. He tells her that it is not right to give the food belonging to the children to dogs. She ignores the insult and tells him that whilst this is true, dogs can at least eat the scraps that fall from the master's table.

Her persistence in the faith that all Jesus needs to do is speak and her daughter will receive freedom from the demon impresses Jesus and he says, "O woman, great is *your faith*! Let it be done for you as you wish." and her daughter recovers within the hour. *(Matthew 15: 21-28)* This woman, as with Abraham and the centurion, understand that God's reality is his word and when he speaks it becomes law and it creates a new reality.

Joshua has the impossible task of defeating the great city of Jericho; a task that in reality is clearly bigger than the Israelites abilities; the wall around the city alone was impenetrable and although they had Jericho in a state of siege, victory seemed impossible. When the Israelites celebrated the Passover, the Lord spoke to Joshua, "I have delivered Jericho and its king into your power," and told Joshua what to do to attain it. God had spoken a new reality, *(it is done)* and Joshua knew this. God had also spoken the instructions on how to do it and this too was a new reality because previously Joshua faced the impossible and could not go further with his campaign.

Joshua believed what he heard and acted upon it although it might have seemed a silly thing to walk around this enormous city for seven days playing a trumpet. It is certain that Joshua instructed the Israelite army as God had spoken and once heard and believed it created a new reality in their minds and a new hope for Joshua's army.

He remained faithful to God's word and persisted in spite of what seemed an impossible reality in the natural, the walls finally collapsed at the sound of the last trumpet blast. With the final blast of faith, the Israelites plundered the great city and captured its king as God had spoken it previously and hence a new reality according to God's Word existed. *(Joshua 6:1-27)*

Because Satan cannot read our minds, he causes us to speak, and when we speak, he can then know our intentions and use them against us. His tactic through temptations is to get us to speak negatively because he knows the power of Jesus' words when he said that by our words we receive condemnation or acquittal. *(Matthew 12: 36 - 37)* Consequently, Satan tries to get us to speak doubt, fear, sickness, loss, anger, bitterness, resentment, curses, and slander in order to destroy. He has no power to speak, so he must get us to do that for him. He fully understands that life and death are in the power of the tongue, and those who love it will eat its fruits. *(Proverbs 18: 20-21)*

Satan uses human speech to destroy in the same way that God uses speech to give life. Consider the power of the spoken word at the consecration of the Eucharist; when the priest speaks the words of Christ, those words become dynamic and what the priest has spoken becomes a new reality; the Body and Blood of Christ.

In the realm of satanic worship, a Satanist will not steal a host from any other church other than Catholic or Orthodox. The Satanist knows as Satan himself does, that

212

these are real priests with the divine authority to consecrate bread and wine into the Body and Blood of Christ. A black mass is a desecration of the true Catholic Mass and it must have a consecrated host in order to defile it; after all, what is the point of defiling a piece of bread. In this way, Satan himself testifies that the Eucharist is really Christ present body, soul, and divinity and that the Word of God when spoken by a priest becomes law and a new reality according to God and the substance of the species changes.

It should not be a mystery why Jesus encourages us to guard our mouth and Saint Paul constantly encourages us to speak good words to each other and not tear each other apart with them; in this regard, prayer is unbelievably powerful and if we pray wrongly, we do not get what we are really seeking. Saint James takes this up very strongly

"Where do the wars and where do the conflicts among you come from. You covet but do not posses. You kill and envy but you cannot obtain; you fight and wage war. You do not posses because you do not *ask*. You *ask* but do not receive, because you *ask* wrongly, to spend it on your passions - Adulterers!" *(James 4:1-4)*

Our prayer must conform to what God has already spoken in order for us to get the result that God and we desire. For us to grasp the enormity of this concept of law, Saint James continues in verse eleven of chapter four, "Do not *speak* evil of one another, brothers. Whoever *speaks* evil of a brother or judges his brother *speaks* evil of the *law* and judges the *law*." This is because God has spoken to us to love one another, to speak good things, encourage, build, and not tear down.

To speak ill of someone breaks the law of God. Likewise, to judge another breaks the law of God by becoming a judge of the law. The opposite of a blessing is a curse and when we speak badly of another, no matter what

213

motive we might have or what justification we give; unspeaking a curse is not possible and so we will not get God's answers to such prayers or needs. On the contrary, we reap a harvest of condemnation upon our own heads according to what we sow.

Chapter 35

The Law of Faith and Love

oth love and faith are laws. When Jesus says that when we break one part of the law we break the whole of the law he is telling us that if we break the law of love we automatically break the law of faith. The same is true if we break the law of faith we break the law of love. When the law of faith and love are broken, hope is gone, and when hope is gone, our reason to live is gone. On the other hand, keeping the laws of love and faith produces hope and a reason to live.

Jesus tells us to be as though we have received (Mark 11:24) if we do this, we already possess the very thing that we asked and hoped for; tomorrow becomes a reality today. Someone once said that a faith that cannot say, I have now, is not faith but wishful thinking. Speaking boldly the promises that God reveals in Scripture about our lives activates the power of that promise into our lives. Faith is a spiritual force that has its origin in God and its end is God himself and all that God desires for us.

In these days, when meditation is so popular, there is great emphasis given on silence, and we cannot deny the need in these stressful times for the peace that comes through silence. To meditate means to think and thinking in silence is paramount as the psalmist said about meditating on the word of God day and night. Teaching on meditation today, much of which is from Eastern mysticism, incorrectly

215

tells us that to "Be still and know that I am God" means to still the mind and empty it. However, "Be still and know that I am God" correctly refers to abiding in the vine, the Word of God, as Jesus taught in John 15. Only then can we produce the everlasting fruit of the Holy Spirit. "If you remain in my *word*, you will truly be my disciples, and you will know the truth, and the truth will set you free." *(John 8:31-32)*

Thinking about the Word, or about Jesus is not sufficient; we must speak the words and do the works as well; both are required to be effective in our lives. Jesus tells us that out of the abundance of the heart, the mouth speaks. When we speak God's promise aloud, it demonstrates our confidence in the promise, our words conform to God's word, and God's word does not return to him void, but accomplishes that for which he sent it.

Actualising God's promises in speech and prayer is very important to possessing the promise. "Why do you call me, 'Lord, Lord,' but not *do* what I command. I will show you what someone is like who comes to me, listens to my words, *acts* on them." Jesus goes on to describe this person as one who built their house on a rock, a house that could withstand a fierce storm, but the one that did not act on his word, met with disaster and Jesus considered them as lacking in wisdom. *(Luke 6:46-49)*

Jesus is emphatic about speaking out the words of faith when he says, "Either *declare* the tree good and its fruit good, or *declare* the tree rotten and its fruit rotten, for a tree is known by its fruit... From the fullness of the heart, the mouth speaks... I tell you on the Day of Judgment people will render an account for every careless word they speak. By your words you will be acquitted, and by your words you will be condemned." *(Matthew12:33-37)* As we have noted

216

previously, these are the words of faith or the words of unbelief that we can speak out without much thought.

Either our expressions of faith will justify us, or our unbelief will condemn us. Once we let a word loose from our mouth, we cannot take it back. *(Proverbs 13:3)* In order for our speech to be positive, our minds need to be conformed to God's word in our hearts. Righteousness means to be in right standing with a king and so righteous speech is to be in right standing with God's Word.

The shield of faith in Ephesians 6:16 is faith working in the heart by love. *(Also 1Thessolonians 5:8)* This is a condition of the heart that gives us right standing with the King. When in right standing with God he answers prayer according to his Word. Because the Spirit and the Word agree, God is pleased to grant our requests according to his promises. We do not live by bread alone, but by every word *(Rhema)* that proceeds from the mouth of God. *(Matthew 4:4)*

Chapter 36

The Word of God acts like Salt

While teaching the first session of our Set My People on Fire seminars, *Knowing the Love of God* in 1994, the Holy Spirit said, "The Word of God is like salt." The understanding from that simple statement has been profound as its meaning was contemplated leading to a revelation of how the Word of God works even in our physical bodies and preserving us for eternal life. The fundamental use of salt is to add flavour and to preserve. The Word of God salts us adding flavour to our lives and subsequently, to those around us but most importantly, it preserves us for eternal life.

Investigating the use of salt revealed some amazing facts. H.R. Malott, chief field representative Salt Institute in the USA recounts that salt appears 30 times throughout the Bible, the history of salt is long with salt used for many purposes in civilisations and religious ceremonies throughout human history. The ancient Greeks used salt to purchase slaves. If a slave were not good quality, people said that "he was not worth his salt" and this is where that common expression began. Jesus came to set the captives free and we are to do the same.

The use of salt as a currency applied to Jesus as the price paid for our redemption. It also applies to us insomuch as we too are to die to self in order to live for another. The ancient Romans also used salt as money. A soldier's payment was in part with salt called *a salarium* from where

218

we get the term *salary*. The Latin word for salt, *sal*, the French words *solde (meaning pay)* and *soldier* are all related. In Italian *soldi* means money, *soldato* is a soldier. In modern times, Ethiopia used salt disks for money kept in a treasury. In several places in Africa, a bride purchased with salt was a common occurrence until recent times.

The earliest known writing on pharmacology published as far back as 2,700 B.C in China called the *Peng-tzao-kan-mu* discussed more than 40 kinds of salt and included descriptions of two methods of extracting it. In 2,200 BC, the Chinese emperor Yu made salt taxes a main source of raising revenue to support the empire.

In England during the late 1700's, the British government did the same when livestock were dying for lack of salt. The tax was so high that riots broke out and finally Parliament abolished the salt tax. During 1930, Mahatma Gandhi marched 200 miles to protest Britain's salt tax that also forbade people from gathering their own sea salt. This event began India's process to independence.

The French salt tax was partially responsible for the French Revolution and the New Assembly ended the salt tax in 1790 to make salt more affordable. There are numerous historical references to the way salt as a currency has played a major role in many civilizations. India, China, Africa and the Middle East civilizations grew around salt deposits.

Salt has also had major military significance. Thousands of Napoleon's soldiers died when retreating from Moscow because there was no salt to heal their wounds. It is interesting that salt was essential for life and healing as is the Word of God. Without salt, healing was not possible and death was the result as well as defeat in battle.

The Word of God gives us life, healing, and victory in our spiritual battles. A more recent military significance was during the American Civil War when the Northern

219

generals attacked the South's salt production because their armies and civilians needed salt to maintain health, tan leather, and preserve food.

Salt used as a preservative is common throughout the ages. In medieval times villages needed to be virtually self-sufficient for their food due to unavailable or poor transport. In Sweden for example, good quality arable land was scarce and used primarily for crops. This meant that the animals, mainly cattle and pigs, grazed in the woodlands. During winter, there was a lack of food to last and so salt preserved the slaughtered animals throughout the winter months.

As a preservative, ancient Egyptians also used salt as a major ingredient to preserve mummies. It was, and still is in oriental countries a practice to use salt to cleanse and harden the skin of newborn babies and we find a reference to this in Ezekiel 16:4. Salt has had such an impact throughout history it is also the subject of fairy tales, stories, fables, and folktales. The term "Take it with a pinch of salt" originated with Charles Dickens ghost story, "To Be Taken with a Grain of Salt." Salt, as with fantasy, myth and historical fact, so too with religious history, for salt has a very significant and crucial role in the life of faith, even to this very day.

A primary source of salt was the Dead Sea or The Salt Sea mentioned several times in the Bible. Because in ancient times there was no way to extract the salt it was difficult to differentiate between the sand and the salt on the shore and so the substance they called salt was mixed both with sand and salt, usually more salt than sand. When there was more sand than salt, they said that it had lost its flavour.

Salt *(sodium chloride)* is essential to life on earth. Most biological tissues and body fluids contain a varying amount of salt. The concentration of sodium ions in the blood relates directly to the regulation of safe body-fluid levels. Salt will draw up the wet blood spilt on cloth or a carpet and help remove the stain.

Coming as I did from a colder climate in England to the often-stifling heat of a Western Australian summer, it was essential to take salt tablets to avoid dehydration caused by sweating that secretes large amounts of salt from the body. 0.9% sodium chloride in water is a *physiological solution* because it is isoosmotic with blood plasma known in medical terms as *normal saline* used in medicine for the prevention or treatment of dehydration. Salt regulates the propagation of nerve impulses by signal transduction.

One of the interesting things about salt is that when it is used it loses itself and so we do not see salt in our food because it makes its contribution and then it is gone. When used in various chemical processes, salt also dissipates after fulfilling its purpose; Salt sprinkled on an icy road melts the ice and vanishes. When the Word of God enters us, it does the same thing and causes us as "the salt of the earth" *(Matthew 5:13)* to make our contribution without drawing attention to ourselves but never the less bring life and healing to the world and the situations around us.

We as salt have the same effect on the world because the Church is what preserves it. When Jesus returns and takes the Church from the earth, and thus the salt removed, there will be nothing left with which to salt it. When this happens, only sin will be left, and the sin will cause the earth to implode, and thus the end will come; because the Word of God has left the earth there will be nothing left to hold it in being. Until that time comes, Jesus tells us, "You are the salt of the earth. But if salt loses its taste, with what can it be seasoned?" *(Matthew 5:13)*

Sodium and chloride that together make salt and gives life, are deadly poisons when separated. The Word of God separated from faith becomes poison insomuch as both require works and without works, faith becomes superstitious beliefs with no substance because without the Word of God it is worthless. The Word of God without works acted on faith becomes an empty religion and gives no glory to God or credibility to the person preaching it; speak the words of the Bible as much as you will, they will have no effect unless united with faith and action.

It is therefore imperative that we understand the importance of reading and understanding the Word of God and by that means, salted with the Word, for the salt of God's Word will have the same effect in us as salt in meat. John 5:24 says, "Amen, Amen, I say to you, whoever *hears my word (Romans 10:10)* and believes *(has faith)* in the one who sent me has eternal life and will not come to condemnation, but has passed from death to life."

And again in John 17:1-3 Jesus reiterates this, "Now eternal life is this, that they should know you, the only true God and the one you sent, Jesus Christ." Jesus prayed regarding us, "Father, they are your gift to me. I wish that where I am they may be with me that may see my glory that you gave me, because you loved me before the foundation of the world." *(John17: 24)*

Salt permeates the fibres of meat when placed in it and preserves the meat beyond its normal term of decay. Because the salt is the active agent it would be true to say that the meat is where the salt is. It is the same with the Word of God in us; we are where the word is. *(1John 4:16-18)* The Word preserves us as the salt preserves the meat, and because the Word is eternal, it preserves us eternally. Jesus rose from the dead and ascended into heaven bodily, and so, where he is, there are we.

We know that in baptism, we have died and risen with him and so it is faith in the Word of God that justifies us and brings us into heaven; we are one with Jesus and therefore one with the Word. "I pray not only for them *(the disciples)*, but also for those who will believe in me through their word, so that they may all be one, as you, Father, are in me and I in you, that they also may be in us, that the world may believe that you sent me." *(John 17:20-21)*

Salt symbolizes immutable incorruptible purity and so the Church values the role of salt and expresses that in its use through various liturgical acts, the baptismal salt and blessed salt are just two examples. Exorcisms also use salt and blessed salt mixed with water.

During a conference a few years ago, a woman came forward for prayer. As the prayer for her blessing began, she became agitated, screamed and ran from the church indiscriminately parting over 800 people pushing them aside as she forced her way to the door. Finally apprehended in the car park, calmed by the team members, she sat in a car awaiting my attention. Arriving at the car it seemed clear that a demon was present and this needed checking against a possible seizure although that did not seem likely.

Before attending to the woman I asked the Lord to show me what to do because I had sensed a spirit of witchcraft and needed wisdom on how to proceed in a public place in full view of neighbours who would not understand what was happening if they saw it. After asking her friend if she had a medical condition, she said no but she had been dabbling in witchcraft and that confirmed my discernment.

I asked the Lord how to proceed because I knew that if she was psychotic and I spoke in English commanding the demon to depart, the woman would understand and react accordingly, and this would not determine that a demon was in fact present; I needed a more certain way to discern it. The Lord spoke and said to pray in tongues. This was because the woman would not understand and therefore could not react; the demon would if one was present. *(1John 4:1-4)* In addition, Saint Paul says that tongues is a sign to unbelievers and this is so because only believers can use this gift of the Holy Spirit; it is the language of the sons of God and God fully understands what they say. *(1Corinthians 14:22)*

The woman was exhausted; head bowed and began to whimper. The speaker at the conference, a priest, had blessed salt the day before and without her knowledge, a small amount placed on her back immediately caused her to sit upright and she began to scowl. After removing idle onlookers that had gathered around, prayer in tongues began as the Holy Spirit inspired and the woman became more agitated.

Now confirmed that a demon was present the tongues became a command for the demon to leave, and with a shudder, it left leaving the woman slumped in the car seat. After a short while, she was aroused and asked how she felt. Relating that she had not felt such peace, she spoke about her involvement with witchcraft. Encouraged to pray for forgiveness she went back into the conference to praise Jesus. Blessed salt played a significant part in the deliverance for this woman.

The Word of God acting like salt in us permeates our whole being and sets us free. The Word of God is eternal, and where the Word is, there are we also. Faith in the Word of God and the application of what it says in our lives brings us liberty, freedom, deliverance, healing, joy and peace. *(James 5:13-15)* In fact, it brings all the promises of God. Moreover, it permeates us with love and gives us hope; a hope that will not disappoint us for it is the very substance of faith and evidence of what we cannot see.

Reading the Bible, listening to good preachers and reading reliable scriptural books salts us with the Word of God, we become tasty and we, as the salt of the earth, preserve it until Jesus returns in glory. "Let your speech always be gracious, seasoned with salt, so that you know how you should respond to each person." *(Colossians 4:6)*

Chapter 37

Your faith can heal your heart and conquer your world

Whatever else we experience in our walk with Christ, the major tests will always be with our faith, and yet it is that very faith that conquers the world. In the natural, this is irksome to our flesh and we seem to seek easy ways for faith to grow, but grace welcomes the challenge and desires to be humbled in order to increase; there is no victory in the world until there is victory in our heart.

Essentially God requires that we crucify the flesh in order to grow in the Spirit. This can be painful and seemingly unloving of God even though he makes it clear that he chastises every son that he receives. It is certain that Peter did not jump with joy when Jesus rebuked him for his lack of faith and told him, "Get behind me Satan! The trouble with you Peter is that you think as men think and not as God thinks." *(Matthew 16:22-23)*

How would you feel if Jesus said that to you? Jesus does not try to comfort Peter but allows him to suffer his betrayal through his denial of Jesus, and this as Jesus looks at him. It also seems cruel that Jesus would later challenge Peter when asking three times if Peter loved him. However, with Peter's yes, Jesus commissions him as the shepherd of his flock. It is unlikely that Jesus doubted Peter's love; after all, Jesus could read men's hearts. The test was for Peter's benefit so that he could know and understand himself.

Many years ago Jesus said, "Eddie. If you want to change the world, change yourself." Since that time, I have taken Jesus seriously at his word and adjusted my attitudes. Due to deep-seated habits however, this has taken a while and that has been frustrating at times. On one occasion very frustrated with failures, I went before God in despair crying, "Lord, please help me. I am so distressed and racked with failure I am in great pain. Every time I begin to walk, I fall over again and I just cannot go on anymore. Lord, please help me!" It is difficult to describe how I felt at that moment except to say that I would rather have died than fail again.

As my whole body went limp with remorse, Jesus spoke to me and said, "My son, all you have to do is get up one more time than you fall." I then understood that the success of the saints was not so much that they do not fall over, but that they got up and kept walking - it is not the amount of times we fall that counts, but the number of times we get up. If we get up one more time than we fall, we stand forever. A person that falls and stays down is a failure but the one that gets up, and keeps getting up, is a walking success. We did not learn to walk the first time we tried as a child but we did eventually; no matter how many times we fell, we finally got it right.

It is the same with the walk of faith and holiness. This walk is difficult at times but it will inevitably overcome many bad habits and there will be clear signs of success, so much so that looking back over the years it will become clear that you are not the same person you once was.

Shortly after conversion, I began to change my habit of profane speech and dirty jokes. Taken aback by a new articulate use of words, people that knew me prior listened more intently and were more open to accept my points of

227

view. Until then, four-letter words described everything. Dropping the use of one particular word caused me to acquire a vocabulary and I became more adept in expression. As a direct consequence of seeing the change in me my staff were convinced of the truth of my message and in a short time, two of them became Catholics and were baptised. Consequently, the atmosphere in the workplace had also changed, for at that time, this was my small sphere of influence in the world and the change in me conquered the circumstance.

Overcoming ourselves in order to have a beneficial influence on the world around us seems to be what Jesus was doing with Peter in a much greater way, for there is no victory in the world unless there is victory in our heart. Peter needed to conquer himself first and because Jesus ordained that Peter should be the shepherd he needed to be challenged the most; he is given much, and much is expected of him, hence the severity of the test. How many aspire to greatness in the Lord but are not willing to pay the price.

Peter recognised Jesus as Christ and due to that, Jesus gave him the Keys of the Kingdom; the power to forgive or retain sin that whatever Peter bound on earth was so in heaven and whatever Peter loosed on earth was so in heaven. These tests were to equip and strengthen Peter when his time came to shepherd the flock as the successor shepherd; without testing and trial, Peter would not be strong enough for the task; Jesus' mission was to the tribes of Israel, but Peter's mission was to the world.

Commissioned to take the Gospel to the whole world, we are to disciple the nations and teach them all that Jesus has said. This is an enormous task and without discipline and the purification of faith, we will not succeed, and the world will conquer us instead. Not all of us can to go to foreign countries, and yet called by God to this same work of grace we can be effective within the sphere of our influence.

As Christians, our field of influence is usually small, generally our immediate family, workplace and a few friends and parishioners and yet, if we are faithful to conquer self in the walk of faith, we can change negative circumstances. Sometimes, our greatest influence is as leaven in the dough. If we were to multiply this by the number of Catholics alone there would be over one billion leavens in the dough of the world; to have an effect on the world we only need to be faithful where we are and in what we do.

Speech of course is not the only thing that we need to have victory in the heart over; we might have the faith to desire, but not have the faith to achieve. Understanding the nature of faith as a seed that needs time to grow we can see that as with the seed it is so with our faith; the potential to produce fruit is in the seed but not the ability until planted, watered and fertilized, only then will it grow and produce fruit in its season. During our seasons of the heart, we need to nurture faith and most often trials and tests provide the fertilizer and the word of God, the living water.

Chapter 38

Faith: The power to forgive - Regardless

The areas of un-forgiveness, resentment, and revenge are bitter roots and dead works that need digging out in the same way as the farmer prepares the soil for planting. To take revenge contravenes the law of love and violates faith because it acts on God's behalf and stands as judge, jury and executioner.

"Beloved, do not look for revenge but leave room for the wrath; for it is written, 'Vengeance is mine, I will repay, says the Lord.' Rather, 'if your enemy is hungry, feed him; if he is thirsty, give him something to drink; for by doing so you will heap burning coals upon his head' Do not be conquered by evil but conquer evil with good." *(Romans 12:19-21)* To do this we do not rely on the other person loving us but on us loving them first, regardless.

When we choose to forgive, we are not condoning the wrong but letting it go and then we are the victors. So many people cannot forgive because their feelings prevent them from doing so. Consequently, they wait until their feelings subside before they even contemplate the idea. In the meantime, they are bound up and sad, often for many years, and in some sad cases, all their lives.

It is no small matter that after teaching the Lord's Prayer, Jesus reiterates the need to forgive otherwise we cannot be forgiven by God, "Unless you forgive another their sins, God will *not* forgive you yours." Also in that prayer it says, "Your will be done on earth as it is in heaven." Now there are two key factors here, God's will, and our will. Jesus says nothing about feeling that we want to forgive but of choosing to forgive.

Choice is an action of the will not the emotions. When we choose to forgive, then God's will done on earth as it is in heaven releases God's eternal forgiveness for us because this is his will. As an action of the will, it still takes faith to forgive and when we act on faith by choosing to forgive, it justifies us and we win.

Now in her early twenties, Melanie grew up not knowing why she was always angry with her mother and at times did not want to live. She left her home in Malaysia and came to Australia to attend university but still without finding happiness.

Eventually she asked her mother why she felt this way. What her mother said shocked Melanie to her soul; because of problems in her marriage, Melanie's mother wanted to abort her when she found out she was pregnant. Melanie said they both cried when she told her but Melanie's feelings of rejection and worthlessness grew to a painful degree from that time.

During the final rally at our 2004 Annual Congress, *"Receiving the Mercy of God,"* Cheryle, one of our intercessors, had shared a vision from God of a baby in a mother's womb with the placenta removed and the child set free. Cheryle said that God was healing someone from the womb. Moved by what she heard Melanie asked for prayer when the call came to do so. "As soon as the prayer began I felt a powerful love touching my heart and I knew it was God." She said. "I had never known love before and it completely overwhelmed me."

231

Melanie said that God's embrace had given her the ability to forgive her mother completely. Failing to hold back tears, she told her story for the first time as Cheryle comforted her. Set free by God's grace Melanie was able to offer mercy to her mother.

After the Congress Melanie contacted her mother in Malaysia and told her for the first time that she loved her. When her mother heard Melanie's forgiveness and words of love, her mother broke down in sorrow. As Melanie shared what God had done for her and how much she loved her mother no matter what she had tried to do, over twenty years of guilt vanished from her mother's heart in a flood of tears.

By God's grace and unfathomable mercy, Melanie's mother found a new daughter and Melanie found a new mother as the grace of forgiveness flowed with healing love. Now both healed and reconciled they have a win-win situation bringing victory for each other because Melanie gained the victory in her own heart first.

Dusty's testimony was also very moving as he shared how he turned from God because of family troubles and began a life of sexual promiscuity and alcohol abuse. After experiencing the Baptism in the Holy Spirit at a Flame Day of Renewal in the remote Western Australian rural town of Perenjori, God began to work in his life. This culminated when Jesus gave him a new heart. "I had asked God to help me and to give me a new heart, but when it happened it was very painful."

God convicted him of his sinful attitudes and as he repented, God's hand appeared to reach into his heart and tore it out replacing it with another completely healed. "It hurt. It really hurt, but God took away my old wounded heart and replaced it with one like his own." *(A new heart I will*

give you and a new spirit I will put within you; and I will remove from your body
the heart of stone and give you a heart of flesh. - Ezekiel 36:26)

Dusty was then able to forgive his father for alcohol and abuse as well as divorcing his mother. He gave up his secular rock band, drugs and sexual encounters and everything else that came with it. He came to Perth, began further studies at university and joined the Flame Music Ministry as a drummer. Dusty's account of God's intervention brought people to tears and that night many others repented and forgave those that had wounded them.

As hard as it seems, forgiveness is a common-sense solution to many ills and depressions; should someone place a burning coal in your hand, what would you do with it? Naturally, you would cast it away as quickly as possible because by not doing so, it would burn deeper and cause more pain and the wound would take longer to heal leaving an ugly scar. This is how it is with un-forgiveness; it burns deeper, causes more pain and leaves a very ugly scar in us. Clearly, the common sense and natural thing to do is to drop it immediately or cast it far away. Even though a burn will still be evident, it will last but a short time and take no time at all to heal and it is doubtless that it will leave a scar.

If God takes our sins and casts then away from himself as far as east is to the west and remembers them no more *(Hebrews 8:12. Hebrews 10:17)* why should we hang on to sin and consequently be cast away with it? If the other person chooses not to change, we are still the victors for they have no more power over us; we have the power and authority to forgive sins and so they do not cling to us. The difference now is that there is an opportunity for the other to change because we have victory over the conflict in our own heart and this is peace in the midst of the storm.

It is easy to love those that love us but there is no merit in that because not loving them would be a sin.

Loving those that hate us is the great trial that perfects our love lived by faith, for it takes faith to love the way that God loves us. Trials produce character and so we count it all joy when various trials come, not because it is so wonderful to experience pain and suffering but because we can now see God working in the situation bringing the victory to those that put their faith in him. *(James 1:2-4)* We are more than conquerors because we do not demand revenge and retribution but grant mercy and seek reconciliation and restoration.

The greatest act of Godly love in a human heart, is to forgive from the heart those that least deserve it. We do not vanquish and oppress our enemy but feed them and set them free because we have the faith to offer mercy as God has offered it to us and because we believe and have faith, we have victory over the world because we have gained a victory over our own heart. It is not so hard because all we have to do is stand fast. If we fall we get up and get going and then, standing one more time than we fall, we stand forever.

The early Christians overcame their own hearts and believed that their faith could conquer the world and within 400 years, it did so without lifting a sword. With the conversion of the Roman Emperor Constantine, the great pagan empire of Rome became the Holy Roman Empire and universally acknowledged Jesus as Lord of lords and King of kings. From that time on, the kings of the earth bowed before the Church to be crowned, and receive the authority to rule in the name of Jesus Christ.

We need to gain this once more in these days as the world turns increasingly away from Christ. This is a great challenge for us, but let us realise that we are the Christians for this age and Jesus has given the ability by the Holy Spirit to contend with it and to overcome it ready for when he returns in glory.

The world is the people close to us within our sphere of influence. If we have a victory over our attitude towards them, then we have victory in the world, and our faith is what conquers the world. We can do this because we are sons of God and this is the character of sons.

"Everyone who believes that Jesus is the Christ is begotten by God, and everyone who loves the father loves also the one begotten by him. In this way, we know that we love the children of God when we love God and obey his commandments. And his commandments are not burdensome, for whoever is begotten by God conquers the world. And the victory that conquers the world is our faith. Who indeed is the victor over the world but the one who believes that Jesus is the Son of God?" *(1John 5:1-5)*

The secret to your liberty, health and personal peace - forgive your father and mother.

Chapter 39

Dokimion - Faith put to the test causes growth

It would be wonderful if life were painless and simple. That would suit most people very well but unfortunately for those that want a wide and easy road to a powerful faith this is not the case. This should not be too hard to understand because life has taught us that we learn many things through pain and difficulties and so it is with the spiritual life of a dynamic faith.

As often said, faith is like a muscle; it needs exercise to grow, and this is true. Exercise is not just flapping our arms loosely at our side, nor with our legs or any other part of the body. In order for a muscle to develop, it needs resistance as we find in weightlifting and other muscle building exercises. Of course, if we only exercise the muscle and not eat, then we will waste away and die. If we only eat and not exercise, we will simply get obese and die. Either way, without a balance of diet and exercise we will be very weak and unhealthy.

It is the same with faith; the food is the Word of God and the exercise is the resistance that we experience when we begin to apply our faith in the Word; as in the physical life, so too in our spiritual and intellectual life. Because the flesh rebels at trials, many take a wider road but others enter the narrow way and excel in faith. The Greek word *dokimion* that means *proved* only appears twice in the New Testament texts in James 1:3-4 and 1Peter 1:6-7 and it refers to faith as "tested" in order to be "proved."

The idea of *dokimion* is from metallurgical chemistry in which a metal, such as gold, melted in a crucible removes impurities and reveal its authenticity. Unless purified by fire, gold retains its potential but only remains a piece of useless ore. Faith too, although containing unimaginable potential, is worthless until put to the test and proved by God, who is a consuming fire.

James begins his letter using the term, "various" trials. The different trials we encounter will conform to the nature of the faith tested, such as our believing faith when challenged with doubts or clever arguments that cause us to question what we say we believe, such as *saving faith* tested when confronting uncertainty regarding our salvation. *Healing faith* tested when we are sick or faith in *God's provision* tested when our material security is threatened.

When persecuted because we are Christian and our faith in the person Christ is tested, will we deny him? When personal tragedy strikes, we might be tempted to denounce God's love and goodness. The various ways in which our faith is tested will always bring us to the fundamental questions of whether we really believe what we profess. We can be confident professing our faith when things go well, but it is another matter when they go awry as we have seen with the disciples in the storm.

Many people pray believing that God hears their prayers, but relying on their feelings they give up believing for the result before the answer comes. Although it sometimes happens, rarely is there an instantaneous result to prayer, especially physical healing. Most of us expect some reasonable delay, but when that delay becomes intolerable and we are ready to give up, that is when faith's trial really begins. At that point, either we slump to the ground as an athlete giving up right at the finishing line or we leap into the unknown in order to see faith work. Perhaps we cannot do that the first time we try, but persistence will inevitably win through and this is where our various trials come in enabling us to grow as we have seen with David previously.

Sandie's daughter suffered severe head injuries in a car accident and even if she survived the coma and lived, the doctors said that due to the extent of the brain damage, severe retardation would result with no hope of recovery. At the same time, her husband lost his job and the mortgage on their home was threatened. Each week Sandie attended our praise meetings filled with joy. As her daughter's condition worsened and the financial problems increased, Sandie remained joyful, which always inspired the other members.

Even in the midst of financial difficulties, they remained faithful to their tithing. Some time later when asked how she could be so joyful when everything was so bad Sandie said, "When Murray and I have no money and we pray for God to provide, I become joyful because I am about to see God work a miracle."

Sandie said the same thing regarding her daughter's full recovery and even as things looked hopeless over the months, Sandie kept her joy. It took many months but today her daughter is well and has no brain damage. Sandie called it "an absolute miracle."

Later, they moved to another state and Murray got another job. They opened a home for wayward girls with their own small income and Sandie's life was under threat many times by the girls that she wanted to help. A year later, a donation to our ministry came from Sandie and Murray with a letter of profound thanks for teaching them about faith in God's unfathomable love; Sandie had won first prize in the State Lotto. God had been faithful to Sandie because Sandie was faithful to God and his Word. None of this happened quickly and so Sandie and Murray's faith was tested in the crucible of personal tragedy and counting all as joy, God was faithful to his promises and Sandie received a healthy daughter and in more ways than one, a healthy pot of gold.

The operation of faith is not dependant on feelings, but on a promise that we choose to accept. *(Hebrews 10:13)* It is certain that Sandie did not feel happy in this situation but she was joyful. Yes, because joy does not depend on feelings either. Both are choices. Sandie chose to be joyful in spite of the problems and her choice to keep her faith carried her through. Saint James says, "Count it all joy when various trials come" not feel it, and that is what Sandie and Murray did, they chose it.

These trials produced character and perseverance. Perseverance was made perfect in the testing, and in the end, they lacked nothing and the resulting happiness was produced by the joy; their faith received "Dokimion"; and stamped, "tested and approved." Throughout those months their faith grew through resistance and was fed on the Word of God showing that faith is the evidence of what we cannot see and the substance of what we hope for, thus demonstrating that Faith + Works = Results.

Saint James says that a faith that has been Dokimion, "proved" produces steadfastness. This also reflects Saint Paul's exhortation for us to "stand fast" when we have done everything we can to stand. Both Saints are in effect saying that when you have done everything you can to break through and all seems impossible, that is the time for the breakthrough!

Steadfastness is the ability to stand no matter what, thriving in confidence and able to face the future in the immovable strength of God. It is in this that faith reaches its full measure and obtains the promises, and God is well pleased because our faith has passed the test and been approved by him. *(Hebrews 12:1-12)* If we choose to believe and follow him, we can expect "Dokimion" because true faith emerges the victor, intact, pure, and dynamic from its trial by fire, for without resistance and the works it requires our faith will wither away. *(1Corinthians 3:10-17)*

Chapter 40

Do not waver

L et us hold *unwaveringly* to our *confession* that gives us hope, for he who made the *promise* is trustworthy." *(Hebrews 10:13)* The promise is trustworthy because the one that made it is trustworthy. There are some 30,000 promises in the Bible and all belong to us by divine decree.

This is an astonishing number when we consider that the average person would not be able name more than ten - at least that is what most of the delegates in our Bible seminars total between them when asked to name them. Without knowledge of the Bible, we remain poor and disadvantaged as a man that attends a banquet and only eats the scraps left because he thinks he has no right to be sitting at the table.

The Gospel is the last will and testament of Jesus Christ of Nazareth and like all last wills and testaments, it must by law, be fulfilled. When we read or hear the Word of God, we are as a family listening to our inheritance and yet for lack of knowledge we perish, for knowledge is the foundation of faith and that knowledge is the Word of God. How can we put our faith in something we know nothing about?

It is essential that we spend time reading the Bible and absorbing its content in order to fulfil its mandate and access the promises that it contains for as we have seen, faith is built on a promise and that reliable promise of God gives the substance of hope; a hope that will not disappoint us.

The Greek word for faith, *pistis* means *a firm persuasion* or *a strong conviction* and so we can read these words into the Bible every time faith is mentioned. There is a fundamental difference between a faith that is fanatical, intellectual or just divine inspiration alone. True faith implies reason to avoid fanaticism or sterile intellectualism.

When saying that we have faith, we are saying that fully persuaded with such a strong conviction we can totally rely on God's promises unwaveringly expecting their fulfilment in our lives. With such a strong conviction, we can hold fast to the truth that all things are possible for the one that believes.

God simply cannot lie and we really need to grab a clear understanding of this, nor does he compromise his Word. John tells us in his first letter that "If we accept human testimony, the testimony of God is surely greater. Now the testimony of God is this that he has testified on behalf of his Son. Whoever believes *(has unwavering faith and firmly convinced by a firm persuasion)* in the Son of God *(Word)* has this *testimony* within him. Whoever does not believe God has made him *(God)* a liar by not believing *(does not have unwavering faith nor firmly convinced by a firm persuasion)* the testimony God has given about his Son. And this is the testimony; whoever possesses the Son has life; whoever does not posses the Son of God does not have life." *(1John 9-12)*

At the end of life, our ultimate desire is to be with God in heaven free from the burden of this valley of tears. Without this hope, life is nothing more than a worthless struggle with short-lived, fleeting moments of peace, success or happiness: a drink and be merry for tomorrow we die attitude. Without hope, our lives are meaningless, and once set, render the reason to live as having no purpose and culminates with self-destruction, lawlessness and suicide. Faith is more than a mere intellectual assent because believing only in the head is not sufficient. Faith in the heart tends towards hope and fills us with love "For a man *believes* with his *heart* and so is *justified,* and he *confesses with his lips* and so is saved." *(Romans 10:10)*

At this point we come right back to the Word upon which this knowledge of God is based for John 5:24 says, "Amen, Amen, I say to you, whoever *hears my word (Romans 10:10)* and believes *(has faith)* in the one who sent me has eternal life and will not come to condemnation, but has passed from death to life." And again in John 17:1-3 Jesus reiterates this, "Now eternal life is this, that they should know you, the only true God and the one you sent, Jesus Christ." The ultimate destination is our own resurrection and attaining the Beatific Vision.

However comprehending our bodily resurrection is beyond us and yet God has shown this with the bodily ascension of Enoch, Elijah, and Mary and through Jesus' ascension, the resurrection. Although there is no record of Moses ascending as with the others, we know that a dispute raged between Satan and God's Archangel Michael over the body of Moses. *(Jude 9)* The fact that Moses appeared with Elijah on Mount Tabor reveals many things to us and not the least is that Moses is alive and appeared in bodily form along with Elijah who ascended into heaven in a fiery chariot. *(2Kings 2:9-11)*

The significance of the Transfiguration has multiple consequences for us and not the least of which demonstrates that Jesus was not Moses or Elijah that had come back as was being said at that time. It also demonstrates that reincarnation is wrong in its concept of everlasting life when stating that Jesus, Elijah, Moses and others, even Buddha and the Hindu deities are a reincarnation of successive avatars.

Fundamentally, the revelation of Hinduism, Buddhism and that of the New Age is that man has forgotten his original state and that true enlightenment is the self-realisation that he is god. For the Christian, revelation is that Jesus of Nazareth is the Alpha and Omega, the first and the last, the Logos and the Rhema, The Word of God and God himself, and through faith in him, we too receive resurrection in the body because his Word acts like salt in us and by faith and grace achieves it.

It is Jesus, God and Incarnate Word that reveals man's true origin and destiny demonstrated in a magnificent way on Mount Tabor since it points to a bodily resurrection and not that of successive migrations of the soul. "I am the resurrection and the life; whoever believes *(has faith)* in me, even if he dies, will live, and everyone who believes in me will never die. Do you believe this?" *(Have unwavering faith, firmly convinced by a firm persuasion) (John 11:25-26. John 3:16)*

The evidence that we are one single being destined by God's will to live forever with one physical body is shown in the fact that we were chosen in Christ before the world *(cosmos)* began and it conclusively refutes reincarnation. "Blessed be the God and Father of our Lord Jesus Christ, who *has blessed* us in Christ with every spiritual blessing in the heavens, as *he chose* us in him *before* the foundation of the world *(cosmos)."* *(Ephesians 13-4)*

Besides, reincarnation also signifies dying constantly in order to be born again into another life and another body. This depends on the law of karma that has more to do with fate rather than faith whereas Jesus says in Luke 20: 38, "He is not God of the dead, but of the living, for to him all are alive." Again, the Bible says, "It is appointed for man once to die and then the judgement." *(Hebrews 9:27)* Our faith in the promises of Christ means that we do not fear judgement because "Hence now there is no condemnation for those who are in Christ Jesus. For the law of the spirit of life in Christ Jesus has freed you from the law of sin a death." *(Romans 8:1-2)*

To stand fast, holding to our faith confession will establish our lives on the cornerstone of Christ. The builders of the New Age and the New World Order have rejected him. But let us, "Come to him, a living stone, rejected by human beings but chosen and precious in the sight of God, and, like living stones, let yourselves be built into a spiritual house to be a holy priesthood to offer spiritual sacrifices acceptable to God through Jesus Christ. For it says in scripture: 'Behold, I am laying a stone in Zion, a cornerstone, chosen and precious, and whoever believes *(has faith)* in it, shall not be put to shame.' Therefore, its value is for you who have faith, but for those without faith: 'The stone which the builders rejected has become the cornerstone,' and 'A stone that will make people stumble, and a rock that will make them fall.' They stumble by disobeying the word, as is their destiny." *(1Peter 2:4-8)*

As for us, we have for our inheritance an unshakable Kingdom so let us not waver until it comes, that is, a new heaven and a new earth because the rock they have rejected as they build their own Babylon towers has become, even more than ever, the most important of all. *(1Peter 2:7, Matthew 21:42-44)*

Jesus is the author, finisher and the one that perfects our faith, he is the high priest of our confession *(Homologia)* and so we have the full assurance that we can accomplish more than we can hope for or imagine for it has not entered our minds what God has prepared in advance. "Amen, I say to you, if you have *faith* and *do not waver*, not only will you

245

do what has been done to the fig tree, but even you say to this mountain, 'Be lifted up and thrown into the sea,' it *will* be done. Whatever you ask for in prayer *with faith*, you *will* receive." *(Matthew21: 21-22)*

Chapter 41

Autarkeia - Faith is our full assurance and self-sufficiency

It is a sad thing to realise that so many Christians opt for so much that is far less than God intended. To them Jesus is there, ever willing to help, but at a distance. From their position, they are content to see themselves as miserable sinners, weak and worthless and yet faith dictates a completely different perspective - one of self-sufficiency, the Greek word for which is *autarkeia*.

This simply means that we have all things in Christ to overcome life's obstacles and are able to release it by our faith confession. *(Colossians 1:27)* We can do this because in him we are new creatures. "Consequently, from now on we regard no one according to the flesh; even if we once knew Christ according to the flesh, yet we know him so no longer. So whoever is in Christ is a *new creation*: the old things have passed away; behold new things have come." *(2Corinthians 5:16-17)*

God has not counted our sins against us but set us free due to Jesus becoming our sin substitute taking upon him the sin of the world. If we can accept what this means, we can be fully assured that if God has not withheld Jesus, he will not withhold anything else either. This means that we can now view ourselves as God does rather than as others might view us or as we might see ourselves.

Being self-sufficient is not an arrogant attitude. Saint Paul was completely self-sufficient and yet he was a humble man. As a faith-filled disciple he understood that to be humble did not mean putting himself down, but rather, having a sober view of the truth. When he did not compare himself as equal with what he called the super apostles, he was not falsely diminishing his worth.

At other times, he would make bold statements about himself, "Although if I should wish to boast, I would not be foolish, for I would be telling the truth." but he was not being prideful; he was being humble accepting that he could accomplish all things in Christ who strengthened him. *(Philippians 4:13)* "But I refrain, so that no one may think more of me than what he see or hears from me because of the abundance of revelations." *(2Corintians 12:6-7)*

In the following verse Paul refers to an angel of Satan sent to beat him should he become too elated. He pleads with God to remove it three times and the only response God gives is, "My grace is sufficient for you, for power is made perfect in weakness." *(2Corinthians 12:9)*

Whilst it is true that our weakness keeps us humble in the face of such an adversary, it is certainly not true that we should lie down and accept it as fate. If that were so, it would negate the truth of Jesus' promise when he said that we could tread on the full force of the enemy *(Luke 10:19)* and our faith would be wavering; there would be no power in our weakness but only defeat.

It is more likely that Jesus was allowing Paul's faith to be tested *(dokimion)* so that in his weakness he would remember the all-sufficient grace that he had freely received as sufficient to beat off Satan's attacks. He did not need Jesus to do this because he already had authority over Satan given by Jesus at the great Commission, "In my name they will drive out demons." *(Mark 16:17)* In addition Psalm 91:13 also held a promise in this regard "You shall tread on the asp and viper, trample the lion and the dragon."

Not understanding this, many Christians live a life of fait accompli when it comes to these matters and accept it as a cross they have no power over, unlike Jesus who conquered his. If we unwaveringly accept these promises of grace and power in our weakness then we could paraphrase Jesus response, "Paul. Why are you asking me to remove this demon? The grace, power and authority given are sufficient to overcome this yourself; the grace given you is sufficient in your weakness." For Saint Paul to do this, he would need to exercise the full assurance of his faith that God could accomplish what he promised when Paul acted upon it. Through this challenge to his faith, Jesus is telling him that in Christ he is self-sufficient because he has God's full assurance of a successful outcome.

Humility is the ability to admit the truth regarding you because anything else is a lie. For many, to say they are not good at something when they are is easier than saying they are good at something when they are.

After a Mass at which I served as an Acolyte one Sunday morning a conversation began between the priest and a couple of parishioners. Father was recounting a game of tennis that he had won the day before saying that his strong point was his backstroke that won the match. One of the women said, "Oh father. You shouldn't boast like that." Father thought deeply for a moment and said in reply, "Well. I am very good, and if I were to say I was not, I would be lying."

His reply was an honest assessment of himself and expressed humility. Unlike father, many people will say they are not as good as they really are at something for fear of boasting and so they can suffer from false humility.

Saint Paul was a humble man but he boldly stated that he was completely self-sufficient; like the God he worshipped, he never put himself down nor claimed to be less than he was; which was the way God saw him. "Not that I say this because of need, for I have learned, in whatever situation I find myself, to be self-sufficient (autarkeia)." (Philippians 4:11, 2 Corinthians 9:8)

Saint Paul had refused to look at things from a natural viewpoint for if he did, it is certain that he would have found much that was lacking and tempted to say those things and reinforce his poverty; he could have looked at his need for provision and *said* I am poor. Rather than speak about his poverty he chose to speak of his provision promised in Christ. This was a way of affirming that he was a new man in Christ and therefore in Christ, he was self-sufficient because the one that made the promise is reliable. *(Ken Chant para)* He had decided to see things God's way regarding money, health and indeed for all his needs; he had God's "full assurance" *(Greek; plerophoria)* that what he believed for, he would receive, and he did.

It is the same for us; we can look at the circumstances as ruling or we can look to the promise as supreme since we too, once receiving Christ become a new creation. As we have said previously, whatever we put our faith in determines the result. We are not alone in our walk of faith "Since we have a great high priest over the house of God, Let us draw near with a true heart in *full assurance* of faith." (Hebrews 10:22)

Because Jesus is our mediator the high priest of our confession, we can have great confidence that he will honour our faith when we speak it and act upon it. "Now he has obtained so much more excellent ministry as he is the mediator of a better covenant, enacted on *better promises*." (Hebrews 8:6)

"For there is one God, there is also one mediator between God and the human race, Christ Jesus, himself human, who gave himself as a ransom for all." *(1Timothy 2:5-6)* "You have not approached that which could not be touched by a blazing fire and gloomy darkness and storm and a trumpet blast and a voice speaking words such as that those who heard begged that no message be further addressed to them. For they could not bear to hear the command: 'If even an animal touches this mountain, it shall be stoned.' Indeed, so fearful was the spectacle that Moses said, 'I am terrified and trembling.'

No, you have approached Mount Zion and the city of the living God the heavenly Jerusalem and countless angels in festal gathering. And the assembly of the firstborn enrolled in heaven, and God the judge of all, and the spirits made perfect, and Jesus, the mediator of a new covenant and the sprinkled blood that speaks more eloquently than that of Abel… Therefore you are receiving an unshakable kingdom." *(Hebrews 12:18-29)*

Faith recognises no failure for if Christ had not atoned for our sins and in heaven, interceding for us at the right hand of the Father our faith would be in vain. *(Hebrews 10:11-22)* It therefore does not entertain the unreliable evidence of feelings or the senses; it rejects everything that is opposed to the Word of God because nothing except God's Word speaks convincingly to faith and the lies and false accusations of Satan have no more power over us. Because we, anchored in Christ, are new creations, we can now view reality God's way with his full assurance, and we too are fully assured and self-sufficient.

Chapter 42

We are stars lighting up the sky

*T*here is no doubt that from a Christian perspective we live in a perverse world where laws legalising sin prevail and Jesus is reviled daily. Yet, it remains true that there is no law against love, peace, joy, self-control, patience, kindness, generosity, and gentleness. *(Galatians 5:22)* We note there is no legislation to make these laws because there is not a law against them.

The bombast of certain artists and writers whose work vilifies Christ and perverts the truth of the Gospel and that of governments that work to remove Christ even from their known history and the theosophical New Age Movement reaches into every area of life with its alternative spirituality and techniques all work to snuff out the light of truth. What was once considered mere superstition has now become acceptable to people in all levels from the man in the street to university professors, governments, corporate executives, scientists, medical practitioners, the UN, and sadly, many Christians, and so God is calling his people to a radical lived faith founded on the living Word of God in order to combat this.

Even the definitive religious practise of yoga either Buddhist or Hindu *(Sanskrit; to yoke with Brahmin)* is now a science as reported on the front cover of Time Magazine during 2004. It is the new marketing position of the East to make it acceptable to the West who seek power and salvation without reference to Christ particularly through science or other none personal inanimate powers.

Yoga has even found a place within the Church and people use it as a prayer technique as faith in the Word of God has waned over the years. It is interesting to note however, that yoga meditation and its positions conform to the character of Hindu deities and through the mantra *(Sanskrit; magic incantation)* calls upon a deity to enter into the one meditating and thus they take on the physical attributes of the spirit they have invoked.

Yoga requires deep breathing and the repetition of a mantra. "A mantra is a sound symbol of one or more syllables often used to induce a mystical state and learnt only from the living voice of a guru and no other way. The user need not understand the meaning of the mantra; the virtue is in the repetition of the sound and said to embody a spirit or deity and, the repetition of the mantra calls this being to the one repeating it. Thus, the mantra both invites a particular being to enter the one using it and creates a passive state in the one meditating to facilitate this fusion of beings." *(Death of a Guru – Rabindranath R Maharaj)*

The term mantra taught in so-called Christian Meditation supposedly means 'prayer word.' The Sanskrit meaning of 'mantra' does not bear this out; words mean what they mean and so a spade is a spade, not a digging implement that could refer to anything from a garden shovel to a bulldozer.

Christian prayer is a personal relationship with God and far from being, as some clerical teachers of mantra prayer in the name of Christian mediation claim, a *prayer technique* or so-called *discipline,* or that it was the way of the Desert Fathers, St. John of the Cross, St. Theresa or Avila and other Catholic mystics. There is no evidence in the lives and teachings of those saints to support such a proposition.

Because the word *mantra* means *to yoke*, people have also taught falsely that this is what Jesus meant when he asked us to take his *yoke* upon us to justify its use.

The mantra and deep breathing exercises open one or more of the seven chakras in order to release the goddess Kundilini. The word *chakra* is also Sanskrit and it literally means *wheel* or *disk* and signifies one of seven basic *(psychic)* energy centres in the body. Each of these centres correlates to major nerve ganglia branching forth from the spinal column. In addition, the chakras also correlate to levels of consciousness, archetypal elements, developmental stages of life, colours, sounds, body functions, and much, much more.

"The name of the goddess Kundilini is symbolised by a serpent with three and one half coils, sleeping with its tail in its mouth. This goddess or "serpent of life, fire, and wisdom" supposedly resides in the body of a man near the base of the spine. When aroused without proper control, it rages like a vicious serpent inside a man with a force that is impossible to resist. Without proper control, the Kundilini will produce supernatural psychic powers having their source in demonic beings and will ultimately lead to moral, spiritual, and physical destruction and Kundilini power is what Eastern meditation and Yoga is to arouse and to control." *(Death of a Guru – Rabindranath R Maharaj)*

All yoga is to release this serpent fire goddess. Call this science if you will, but it will not stop its original function and this is the great deceit of the *science* of yoga. Even that used only for physical relaxation *(hatha)* requires an induced meditative state achieved through deep breathing exercises and the use of a mantra, and this is all part of the new consciousness raising of the psychic faculties in order to accept a new world religion and international political world governance.

Also there is a resurgence of ancient beliefs in the elemental spirits, witchcraft, Wicca, Creation Spirituality, occult metaphysics such as the Silva Method of Mind Control, Satanism, the horoscope, alchemy, magic, neo-Gnosticism, humanism, all things mystically Eastern that originate in the earliest religions of fallen man and so much more that it would take another book to document it all.

In these last days, the devil is once more blinding the minds of unbelievers that are becoming increasingly anti Christ. With the supposed dawning of the Age of Aquarius, they declare Christ as no longer relevant because all truth is relative for the age Pisces has passed. "Age of Aquarius: each astrological age of about 2146 years is named according to one of the signs of the zodiac, but the "great days" goes in reverse order, so the current Age of Pisces is about to end, and the Age of Aquarius will be ushered in.

Each age has its own cosmic energies; the energy in Pisces has made it an era of wars and conflicts. But Aquarius is set to be an era of harmony, justice, peace, unity etc. In this aspect, New Age accepts historical inevitability. Some reckon the age of Aries was the time of the Jewish religion, the age of Pisces that of Christianity, Aquarius the age of a universal religion." *(A Christian reflection on the "New Age" Pontifical Council for Culture Pontifical Council for Interreligious Dialogue)*

With this revival of the occult zodiac, many that once professed faith in Christ have also turned to faith in the planets including 'mother earth' as the erroneous doctrine of so-called Creation Spirituality demonstrates and we can find this very daunting. This quote from an article by Srinivas R. Ranga in the India Worldwide magazine, 9/30/1995 illustrates this situation - "VEDIC ASTROLOGY IS IT GOING TO BECOME UNIVERSAL? After the "invasion" of the West by the two main elements of Hindu way of life - yoga and ayurveda - now it's the turn of Vedic astrology. It has made rapid strides in the West.... For the last few years, it has attracted many a westerner to its fold. There are a number of foreigners who have embraced this ancient art of predicting or determining the influence of the planets and stars on human affairs, based on the Vedas, the Vedanta..."

One day there was jumble sale in Hell. Satan was selling off at a bargain basement price all the sophisticated tools that he uses to trap man into sin and depravity. All the minor demons eager to be as effective as their master stumbled over each other, as do shoppers awaiting the annual sale to open, dashing in with abandon to grab what they can before someone else gets it as the doors are flung open. Trampled under foot of bigger demons, a small demon whose height only allowed him to see at the level of the tabletop struggled unsuccessfully to see what he could grab.

Fighting his way along he suddenly spied an object hidden between all the sophisticated paraphernalia. Reaching out he grabbed the object. To his astonishment, it was just a triangular shaped piece of metal; it had no flashing lights, buttons or working parts. Bewildered by this strange find, he approached Satan sitting on his throne, "Master. I have just found this. What is it?" Immediately Satan grabbed it and said, "You cannot have that!" Now the little demon begged the question, "Hey, you are selling off all this amazing stuff and you do not even care if you do not get paid for it, but this you will not let go. What is so important about this little wedge?" Satan replied, "This is all I need." The little demon said, "Then, what is it? Satan replied, "It is called, discouragement."

Without faith, we will always become discouraged when we face mountainous obstacles in our lives and most especially with laws that in effect make sharing the Christian message openly unacceptable behaviour. This will be even worse if we are ignorant of the Word of God upon which true faith is the foundation. In the face of such opposition, it is understandable to feel afraid of the task appointed us by Jesus in the Great Commission. Yet, rather than worshipping the stars, we, who once fell as if stars are by faith called to be light to the nations.

Archbishop Hickey of Perth, Western Australia challenged delegates at our "Entering the Mysteries of Light Congress saying, "You must shine among them like stars lighting up the sky. *(Philippians 2:5)* I must ask this of you and of myself; how we can live up to this? Yet, expected of us, we are to live among evil and change it, not compromising it. The effect of God's light would make us free people, healed of spiritual and physical pain and injury as well experiencing God's peace and adoption as God's children."

The Archbishop also asked why people were Catholic or Christians. "Was it a habit or was it conversion? Have you made a choice to accept Jesus? Have you experienced that journey from death to life, to freedom and to the light?" Perhaps we need to answer that vital question before finishing this book.

Saint Paul reaches over the centuries to assist us in our struggle when he says, "Therefore, since we have this ministry through mercy shown to us, we are *not discouraged*. Rather, we have renounced shameful, hidden things; not acting deceitfully or falsifying the word of God, but by the open declaration of the truth, we commend ourselves to everyone's conscience in the sight of God. And though our gospel is veiled, it is veiled for those who are perishing *(Revelations 21:8)* in whose case the god of this age has blinded the minds of unbelievers, so that they may not see the light of the gospel of the glory of Christ, who is the image of God. For we do not preach ourselves but Jesus Christ as Lord, and ourselves as your slaves for the sake of Jesus for God

257

who said, 'Let light shine out of darkness,' has shone in our hearts to bring to light the knowledge of the glory of God on the face of Jesus Christ. But we hold his treasure in earthen vessels that the surpassing power may be of God and not from us." *(2Corinthians 4:1-7)*

No, we do not worship the stars nor the earth but the one that placed them there because we posses the prophetic message that is altogether reliable, "You will do well to be attentive to it, as to a lamp shinning in a dark place, until day dawns and the morning star rises in your hearts." *(2Peter 1:19-21)* Jesus is the bright morning star that rises in our hearts and we are to shine in the same way, "I, Jesus, sent my angel to give testimony for the churches. I am the root and offspring of David, the bright morning star." *(Revelations 22:16)*

The purpose of faith is to give glory to God and our faith removes the veil of corruption and brings us hope, "Therefore, since we have such hope, we act very boldly and not like Moses, who put a veil over his face so that the Israelites could not look intently at the cessation of what was fading. Rather, their thoughts were rendered dull, for to this present day the same veil remains unlifted when they read the old covenant, because through Christ, it is taken away... but whenever a person turns to the Lord, the veil is removed. Now the Lord is the Spirit, and where the Lord is, there is freedom.

All of us gazing with unveiled face on the glory of the Lord are being transformed into the same image from glory to glory, as from the Lord who is the Spirit." *(2Corintians 3:12-18)* Now when asked what my star sign is, I simply reply, "The Bright Morning Star."

Chapter 43

Our "Yes" to God is our Great Amen of faith

Through faith, what was lost in Adam now belongs to us in Christ. We, like Saint Paul, have not seen Jesus in the flesh as did Mary and the other Apostles, and so Paul is the perfect example of faith that believes without seeing and his life is the evidence of that; his whole life is one big yes to God. He also demonstrates the hope; the confident expectation of everything good from God that faith brings. He declares to us throughout the ages that everything is possible because we too have God's full assurance to make us self-sufficient through Christ and his Word.

In order to live a life of faith we must of necessity, accept that the promises of Christ apply to us no less than they did to Saint Paul, Mary and all the Apostles, otherwise we will not find hope in the full assurance of the message because as we have noted, faith is taking God seriously at his Word.

The word Amen is an ancient Hebrew oath that indicates being - He who is. It is an affirmation of being that is Jesus: He who is. Amen as an oath means, God supports what I say. Amen means, "Let it be done", or, "It is done." Amen is the final word that includes all others spoken in prayer and completes them; it is the most powerful of faith-statements we can ever speak; it is an irrevocable "yes, it is done!" No other option is entertained because the next step is to act upon it as an absolute fact because we already posses what we have said yes to. The fact that our "Amen" is said at the end of a prayer expresses absolute faith that what has been said or asked for is a reality before it appears.

The distance between amen and when the result comes is the measure of faith in human time. It is the meanwhile in which we grow in wisdom and it perfects our patience as we live each moment with a confident expectation of the good we have asked God for because faith has its due season, and as certain as summertime and harvest, it will come. *(Galatians 6:9-10)*

The most powerful and miraculous faith "yes" ever spoken from human lips was from that of Mary when she took God at his word through the Archangel Gabriel saying, "Let it be done to me according as your word." *(Luke 1:38)* Even though in the natural she could not see how it was possible to bear a child, Mary's faith "yes" welcomed the Word that came from God and the Word became flesh and born of her.

Had Mary wavered with a half-hearted acceptance it is doubtless that the miracle of the Incarnation of the Word of God would have occurred as it did. Because of Eve's rejection, Mary's acceptance was imperative to the restoration that God promised in Genesis 3:15 because it depended entirely on a freewill to grant him permission to act. Mary humbly submitted her free will, not because she had proof or evidence, but because she had faith in God's Word and that justified her faith and the consequence of that is our salvation and justification through faith in her son, Jesus.

Everything regarding faith is our "yes" to God no less than it was for Mary now a woman clothed with the sun and the stars at her feet. *(Revelations 12:1)* Our "Yes" believes without seeing. It agrees with God because it is Christ's guarantee that all the promises are reliable and that they are complete in anyone that believes in them. Can we say "yes" salvation is ours, healing is ours, provision is ours, can we say "yes" every spiritual blessing in the heavens is ours. Can we say yes because our "yes" is our great amen, and although it seemed as one small step for Mary, it was a giant leap for humanity! When we can personalise this "yes", this "Amen", it entertains no doubts that everything God has said regarding us is true.

If we can say, "Yes" as Mary did, we can truly say without doubt, that our faith is the *evidence* of what we cannot see, and the *substance* of our hope. We will *know* by faith that the universe is in fact created by the Word of God, so that what is visible came to be through the invisible and to us, the mystery revealed fully and the veil removed and we can see clearly that the heavens show forth the glory of God and creation sings his praise.

Chapter 44

From New Age to New Faith:
My Personal Testimony

Religion was not high on the list of my priorities during my adolescence in England. Although my mother was a Catholic, she did not practice her faith for reasons that I do not know even to this day.

The only reason seemed to be that my father, although a wonderful man was a non-practicing Christian from a Scottish Anglican background and he did not go to church. My mother was an Irish Catholic and these unions were not acceptable in those days especially in the poor working-class areas of Birmingham where we lived, and so the idea of religion did not seem to have any appeal and especially so after reaching puberty.

Before that, Jesus was a childhood companion. My father was a keen angler winning many prizes that furnished and adorned our home. He would take me fishing with him each Sunday during the summer months, and as I played in the fields, a young man who I now know to be Jesus would often come and walk with me.

On one beautiful summer day when I was about four years old, he came to me while playing in a wheat field. He took my hand and we walked together in silence picking the seeds of wheat. I did not see his face and only remember the strong tanned hand and the brilliance of his long garment. Although filed away in my mind over time, the sense of security and love has never left my memory.

Leaving school at age fifteen, I began a career in graphic arts eventually becoming very successful. I also began playing the guitar. My band, the Creatours, became very popular around England and shared gigs with chartbusters like The Moody Blues, Searchers, Kinks, Peter and Gordon, Stevie Winwood, the Spencer Davis Group, Buddy Holly's band The Crickets and many others during the days of the Merseyside and Brum-Beat *(Birmingham)* music revolutions.

Throughout the years, and especially after leaving the band and migrating to Australia at the height of the Hippie movement, concentrating more on art, and eventually owning my own studio and several other businesses, an interest in astrology as described in chapter six, as well as theosophy, Hinduism, and yoga grew strong. Along with the assistance of marijuana *(tripping grass)* and hashish, the so-called religious experience using yoga and drugs became a part of daily life and with it, a fascination with tantric yoga and drugs in combination for sexual pleasure.

All things mystical were an attraction and at one time, whilst living with a young woman who practiced witchcraft, the idea of becoming a warlock became a great attraction. With the added experience of astral flight *(out of body experiences)*, it became more convincing by what seemed to be the truth when an experience of levitation, which I now know was caused by a demon, occurred one night.

During those days, dark spirits called Shades would appear when falling asleep and after painful paralysis, took the soul to strange places. Consequently, the works of Edgar Casey who consulted the Karmic Records whilst in a yogic trance to find cures for sickness, as well as other occultists became a foundation of knowledge to understand this and so an interest in the Hindu Bhagavad-Gita, Upanishads, and the Rig Vedas fed the idea of astrology that eventually governed each day.

Other chemical stimulants such as those now called *speed*, along with alcohol, hashish or marijuana would keep the party going for days, usually from Wednesday to Sunday with little or no sleep. The idea of meeting Jesus was a frightening concept. Due to a sense of guilt, I believed that to encounter him literally meant death and going to hell, consequently, the Bible did not feature in this spirituality.

Influenced as a child in England by the prejudice against Catholics, it became almost a mission as an adult to convince Catholics that they were hypocrites and I seized any opportunity to do so, inevitably finding my mark as does a snake spitting its venom with unrestricted enthusiasm.

By this time, life was full with commercial success and popularity along with the respect that good art and talent stimulated from my peers in the advertising industry. Never the less it was all these things that dominated daily life and values and a typical week would be going to a night club on Wednesday and using drugs to remain awake until Sunday morning when sleep would lull away hangovers and prepare for Monday's work - but all this came to an abrupt end one Sunday morning.

Arriving home from the clubs around 6am, my body collapsed and fell motionless and paralysed on the lawn. Although unable to move, my mind was alert and knew that death was present. At my right, a menacing dark pit appeared, and knowing exactly what it was, the pulse of life in my body and soul was slowly seeping into it like a black liquid. I knew I was dying and judging by the nature of the pit, going to hell and at that moment the gods of astrology, the New Age, the occult, and mysticism could not save and I knew it as a far greater reality than any other reality I had known until then. In desperation, my soul cried out, but not to the now impotent gods in whom I had put my faith and trust until then, but to an unknown God that must be better and more able to save.

In the silent unfathomable screams of desolation, I cried out to speak to the one that was above all these known gods if there was one, desperately eliminating any concept that I had known until then; as much as I was trying to escape the pit, I was also escaping the gods that put me there. The idea of dying and going to hell knowing the truth was by now of far greater importance than to live one moment longer without it and I was prepared to accept that possibility to find it.

This horrendous agony continued for some time and when it seemed as if life, like the last grains of salt leaving the upper chamber of a an hour glass was slipping for all eternity into darkness, it changed.

Overcome and bombarded by an indescribable love it immediately revealed my abject shame and that caused me to reject it, but the stronger the resistance, the stronger the love became until finally it was accepted.

At that moment, immersed *(baptised)* in a love so powerful it is impossible to describe, a great peace flooded my soul as the pit into which it was falling closed. At that moment, I knew God was real and that he was Love and this love was not the same as the peace of the gurus I had come to believe in, but a person whose name at that time, I did not know. Falling asleep, I awoke some hours later and went to bed.

Although I now had this knowledge of God's love, not much had changed – that was until an encounter with a young Catholic girl in a bar some months later - all the best efforts to convince her of the futility of her faith failed. She knew little about anything except that she was a Catholic and that was very infuriating.

Because of this encounter, I began to read a Bible given to me by a woman at my local grocery store after I told her about my levitation experience. She said it would keep the evil spirits away as I fell asleep - it is in the twilight zone between waking-consciousness and sleep that the evil spirits (*Shades*) would appear. I had not paid much attention to her nor the Bible, but had left it open at the bedside anyway.

That Bible had been there for over nine months when I finally looked into it that night with a firm decision to see what it said without judging.

As I read from the beginning of Matthew in the old King James language, I was unimpressed by what were to me childish stories about baby Jesus; I loved Christmas of course, but this was just too much to bear at my age and so-called sophistication (*I was very cool*) at the time.

When reading the Gospel of Matthew a few weeks later a flash of light pierced my mind and suddenly I *knew* this Jesus was alive! He was real and I recognised him as the young man in the wheat field as a child.

In that instant I knew but did not know how I knew, nor did I know what I knew, I just knew and that was the truth and the clearest reality ever experienced as it transcended and annihilated all previous knowledge.

"Indeed, the word of God is living and effective, sharper than any two-edged sword, penetrating even between the soul and spirit, joints and marrow, and able to discern reflections and thoughts of the heart. No creature is concealed from him, but everything is naked and exposed to the eyes of him to whom we must render an account." (*Hebrews 4:12-13*) Then as I read that no one could know the Son unless the Father reveals him and no one came to the Father except by Jesus, the God with no name now had one; his name is Jesus.

Now it all made sense. "Since you have purified yourselves by obedience to the truth for sincere mutual love, love one another intensely from a pure heart. You have been born anew, not from a perishable but from an imperishable seed, through the living and abiding word of God." *(1Peter 1:22-25)*

Now a Christian I could not keep this good news to myself and like cold fat hitting a hot pan, did not miss an opportunity, because no matter the cost. "I am not ashamed of the gospel: It is the power of God for the salvation of everyone who believes, for in it is revealed the righteousness of God from faith to faith; as it is written, 'The one who is righteous by faith will live.' " *(Romans 1:6. Para)*

At the first opportunity for sharing the experience with colleagues and clients at the advertising agency that I did freelance work for, they viewed me with pity due to what seemed to them as over enthusiastic postulations.

At the clubs and pubs, I took every opportunity to tell people about Jesus and it was on one such occasion, bouncers, as previously mentioned, beat me for talking about him.

Thomas A Kempis, John of the Cross, Theresa of Avila, Francis, Augustine, Aquinas and many great saints became my first exposure to Catholic spirituality. Through them, I discovered that what I understood about the Eucharist from reading the Bible was the same, and a deep desire to meet Jesus there became a painful experience because I was not a Catholic and could not receive the Eucharist in Holy Communion. I would go to Mass and weep with my hands hiding my face when everyone went to communion, and mistakenly, many people thought I was very holy due to this. Eventually I was able to join the Church and recieved my Confirmation at the Benedictine Abbey in New Norcia, 75kms north of Perth in Western Australia.

Since then faith has become the lived experience of what I believe in Christ and what I have come to believe about me through him. I am still coming into knowledge of Christ through prayer and his Word and certainly still growing in holiness.

Although I still fall short of the ideal and the perfection I would aspire to attain, it is my faith in Jesus that keeps me going - when I fall, I get up, and get going. If I fall again, I get up and get going again; my faith in God's unconditional perfect love gives me courage to keep moving on no matter what hinders or how hard it might seem and that was certainly the case when diagnosed with prostate cancer as previously mentioned. Saying 'yes' to God's promises every day for two years as the visible evidence of the cancer grew, the *evidence* of the *promise* of healing *that I could not see* was far greater. After eight biopsies, the result was negative and ten years after, tests are still clear.

Faith in Jesus as Lord gives me the courage to love in spite of someone not loving me and in time, I learnt to forgive from the heart as soon as an offence occurred and to forgive totally those that have abused me in so many different ways throughout my life.

Faith gives me the courage to love myself as Christ does even though I become frustrated at times and want to give up as I strive to understand these mysteries by the grace of God and live by them.

Faith gives me the courage to accept God's call to be an Evangelist, live by divine providence and even to write this book, for without faith, fears and inabilities would overwhelm me to the point of running away and doing something seemingly safer, secure and more convenient.

Through these things, I recognise my weakness, and therefore the need for the steady hand of God to support me in all I do and to lift me from the dust into which I can often fall. Moreover, faith reveals the presence of God, and although he is invisible to my eyes, he is never the less visible to my faith and reflected in all that he has made.

Perhaps the next time you are tempted to check your horoscope, you might look up at the stars in the sky instead, and there you will see visible evidence of an invisible God and his plan in Christ for you in magnificent splendour displayed in all its glory for you to see.

God's dwelling place is with man and this is for our great comfort as we face the seemingly immovable mountains that life can throw in front of us as we try to move ahead - placing our faith in natural things is folly indeed for nothing except the Word of God will last forever.

"Behold, God's dwelling place is with the human race." He says that the old order has passed away, that the one that sat on the throne makes all things new, and that Jesus is the Alpha and the Omega, the first and the last promising life-giving water. *(Revelation 21:1-7)*

All creation and especially the universe give testimony to Jesus as Lord. Shown in its construction, order and sequence placed there by God, are now clear by the Hebrew names and the continuity of all the languages we have looked at.

As we have seen by studying the names of the constellations, they all testify to the truth that God's Word placed all in their position according to the plan set forth before the world began to complete all things in Christ.

We also understand by the Word of God, that in all wisdom and insight, he has made known to us the mystery of his will in this regard *(Ephesians 1:8-10)* and this is how we know by faith in God's Word that this is so. "He is the image of the unseen God and the first-born of all creation, for in him were created all things in heaven and on earth: everything visible and everything invisible, thrones, dominations, sovereignties, powers – all things were created through him and for him. Before creation, he existed, and he holds all things in unity.

Now the Church is his body, he is its head. As he is the Beginning he was first to be born from the dead that he should be first in every way; because God wanted all perfection to be found in him and all things to be reconciled through him and for him, everything in heaven and everything on earth, when he made peace by his death on the cross." *(Colossians 1:15-20)*

It is certain that even with the dawning of the Age of Aquarius being a new world religious epoch drawn from the occult understanding of the zodiac that rejects Christianity, it will not be able to eradicate the truth from the very stars used to predict it. When understood from God's Word that underlies the corrupt use of the constellations, the very stars themselves testify that Jesus is Lord and that is clear for all to see; the universe speaks only of his glory and our ultimate victory in Christ.

"The New Age appeals to people imbued with the values of modern culture... It 'does not demand any more faith or belief than going to the cinema.'" *(A Christian reflection on the "New Age" Pontifical Council for Culture Pontifical Council for Interreligious Dialogue)*

As you ponder these mysteries, let gratitude well up in your heart giving praise to God, for praise is the language of faith and the language of the children of God and *all creation* is groaning in the pangs of childbirth for the revelation of his sons. *(Romans 8:19)*

Faith is what keeps us going from the moment we accept Christ and his salvation giving us the ability to live it and bring it to fruition throughout life. It is also our ability to believe that the impossible is possible, and then to go about achieving it, and faith, invisible by its nature, is visible when it reflects our deeds.

Faith is a miracle in itself: saying *yes* to God saved me, and so I can say without doubt, "Blessed be the God and Father of our Lord Jesus Christ who in his great mercy gave us a new birth to a *living hope* through the resurrection of Jesus from the dead. To an inheritance that is imperishable, undefiled, and unfading, kept in heaven for you who by the power of God are *safeguarded through faith* to a salvation that is to be revealed in the final time." *(1Peter 1:3-5)*

Therefore, as God *is*, so *is* faith, it is a gift of God supernaturally infused by him and certainly an unwarranted or unearned favour called Grace. It can accomplish all things through Christ in whom it has its origin for it reveals all mysteries by his Word.

Faith is a miraculous gift of God that can accomplish everything that God said. Moreover, the greatest miracle that faith accomplishes is salvation, especially for those that least deserves it and God's plan written in the stars really does reveal our true destiny in Christ.

It is certain that as you have been reading these chapters, your faith, although it might have faced a challenge, has never the less grown along the way and that has been the real object of this book. As you begin, or continue your journey of faith, it will continue to take you boldly where no man has gone before.

As you begin to understand that your faith really is the realisation of what you hope for and the evidence of things you cannot see, and that by faith you can understand that the universe was indeed ordered by the word of God so

271

that what is visible came to be through the invisible - the truth will set you free. And through all this, either by faith in the Word of God, or by science, you will give glory to the Father and to the Son and to the Holy Spirit because as it was in the beginning, it is now, and ever shall be; a world without end in a beautiful universe created by the Word of God. *(2Peter 3ff)*

New American Bible
> Catholic Bible Press
> A division of Thomas Nelson Publishers Nashville USA

Catechism of the Catholic Church
> Geoffrey Chapman. Villiars House, 41/47 Strand, London WC 2N
> 5JE

Aquinas Shorter Summa
> Sophia Institute Press – Manchester, New Hampshire,
> NH 03108

A Christian reflection on the "New Age"
> Pontifical Council for Culture Pontifical Council for Interreligious
> Dialogue
> www.vatican.va/roman_curia/pontifical_councils/interelg/docum
> ents/rc_pc_interelg_doc_20030203_new-age_en.html

Paraphrases: Faith Dynamics by Ken Chant
> Vision College Ltd. GPO BOX 2693 Sydney NSW Australia 1980

Paraphrases: Salt and Christianity
> H.R. Malott Chief Field Representative Salt Institute circa 1970
> www.saltinstitute.org/pubstat/malott.html

Paraphrases: Dr. Chuck Missler
> Mazzaroth - Testimony of the Stars on Audiotape
> Koinonia House Inc., P.O. Box D, Coeur d'Alene, ID 83816

Paraphrases: The Witness of the Stars
> E. W. Bullinger London 1893
> http://philologos.org/__eb-tws/default.htm

12 Steps to Divine Healing (ISBN: 0-646-30706-1)
> Eddie Russell FMI © Flame Ministries International PO BOX 8133
> Subiaco East, Western Australia 6008

The Set My People on Fire Seminars
    © Flame Ministries International POX 8133,
    Subiaco Western Australia 6008

What's in a Word
    Eddie Russell FMI - Blaze Magazine Online
    www.flameministries.org/word.htm

Death of a Guru
    Rabindranath R Maharaj.
    Holman Bible Publishers, Nashville

The New Catholic Encyclopaedia
    www.newadventorg/cathen/a.htm

School of Mathematics and Statistics
    University of St Andrews, Scotland
    www-history.mcs.st-
    andrews.ac.uk/Mathematicians/Eudoxus.html

Consider the Heavens
    Peter Tillet. New Holland Publishers (Australia) Pty. Ltd.

Mazzaroth: From the Alpha and the Omega
    Introduction by Jim A. Cornwell, Copyright © 1995
    www.mazzaroth.com/Introduction/MazzarothDefined.htm

Greek, Hebrew and Arabic translations:

Oxford Dictionary of the Bible by W.R.F. Browning
    Oxford University Press, 1996

W.E. Vine's M.A., Expository Dictionary of New Testament Words
    Published 1940

New Advent Catholic Encyclopaedia
    www.newadvent.org/cathen/09328a.htm

Strong's Exhaustive Concordance of the Bible
    With Hebrew, Chaldee and Greek Dictionaries
    Riverside Book and Bible HouseIowa Falls, Iowa 50126

Testimony of the Stars
     Dr Chuck Mizzler

Mazzaroth: From the Alpha and the Omega
     Jim. A. Cornwell

The Witness of the Stars
     E. W. Bullinger - London 1893

Glossary References
New Advent Catholic Encyclopaedia

Hylomorphism:

> hylo-, "wood, matter" + -morphism < Greek - morph, "form") is a philosophy that highlights the significance of matter in the structure of being, regarding matter as important (or even more so) as form - Metaphysical view according to which every natural body consists of two intrinsic principles, one potential (namely, primary matter) and one actual (namely, substantial form). It was the central doctrine of Aristotle's philosophy of nature. He based his argument for Hylomorphism chiefly on the analysis of change. If a being changes (e.g., from being cold to being hot), something permanent must exist that remains throughout the change; in addition, there must be an actual principle that differentiates the earlier from the later state. The permanent principle is matter, the actual principle form.

Cosmogony:

> By this term is understood an account of how the universe *(cosmos)* came into being (gonia - gegona = I have become). It differs from cosmology, or the science of the universe, in this: that the latter aims at understanding the actual composition and governing laws of the universe as it now exists while the former answers the question as to how it first came to be. The Christian Faith accounts for the origin of the universe by creation ex nihilo of the matter, out of which the universe arose, and the

preservatio, or maintenance, of Providence according to which it developed into what it now is.

Modern science has propounded many theories as to how the primeval gaseous substance evolved into the present harmony of the universe.

These theories may be called scientific cosmogonies; and the account of the origin of the world given in Genesis, 1 and 2, is styled Mosaic cosmogony. The word cosmogony however, is usually applied to mythic accounts of the world's origin current among the peoples of antiquity and the more modern races, which have not been touched by recent scientific methods.

Cosmology:

From its Greek etymology (kósmos world; lógos, knowledge or science) the word cosmology means the science of the world. It ought, therefore, to include in its scope the study of the whole material universe: that is to say, of inorganic substances, of plants, of animals, and of man himself. ...In fact, the wide range indicated by the etymology of the word has been narrowed in the actual meaning. In our day, cosmology is a branch of philosophical study, and therefore excludes from its investigation whatever forms the object of the natural sciences.

While the sciences of physics and biology seek the proximate causes of corporal phenomena, the laws that govern them, and the wonderful harmony resulting there from, cosmology aims to discover the deeper and remoter causes which neither observation nor experiment immediately reveals. This special purpose restricts in many ways the field of cosmology.

There is another limitation not less important. Man's unique position in the universe makes him the object of a special philosophical study, viz. psychology, or anthropology; and, in consequence, that portion of the corporeal world with which these sciences deal has been cut off from the domain of cosmology properly so-called.

Metaphysics:

The word metaphysics is formed from the Greek meta ta phusika, a title which, about the year A.D. 70, was related by Andronicus of Rhodes to that collection of Aristotelean treatises which since

276

then goes by the name of the "Metaphysics." Aristotle himself had referred to that portion of philosophy as "the theological science" (theologikê), because it culminated in the consideration of the nature of God and as "first philosophy" (prôtê philosophia), both because it considered the first causes of things, and because, in his estimation, it is first in importance.

The editor, however, overlooked both these titles, and, because he believed that that part of the Aristotelean corpus came naturally after the physical treatises, he entitled it "after the physics." This is the historical origin of the term. However, once the name was given, the commentators sought to find intrinsic reasons for its appropriateness. For instance, it was understood to mean "the science of the world beyond nature", that is, the science of the immaterial.

Again, it was understood to refer to the chronological or pedagogical order among our philosophical studies, so that the "metaphysical sciences would mean, those which we study after having mastered the sciences which deal with the physical world" (St. Thomas, "In Lib, Boeth. de Trin.", V, 1). In the widespread, though erroneous, use of the term in current popular literature, there is a remnant of the notion that metaphysical means ultra physical: thus, "metaphysical healing," means healing by means of remedies that are not physical.

Hexaemeron:

Hexaemeron signifies a term of six days, or, technically, the history of the six days' work of creation, as contained in the first chapter of Genesis.